Keep The Light Burning!

Devotionals for Patriots

Dr. Perry Greene

Perry Greene has devoted his life to ministry, both in local churches and now in *God-N-America*. He has courage and is highly informed. Put another way, Perry Greene "gets it." And like many of the heroes of Christian history, he has paid a price for sharing the truth. He sees what is happening and can guide you on how to respond. Simply stated, when Perry speaks, listen. When Perry writes, read. As a "Patriot Pastor," he reconnects God and America by telling His story in our history. *'Keep The Light Burning!'* informs, inspires, and engages Patriots to take up God's cause of Liberty in the 2 Chronicles 7:14 tradition.

- Dr. Jim Garlow, CEO, Well Versed

DEDICATION

This book is dedicated to all American Patriots who want God's will to be done on earth as it is in heaven.

CONTENTS

ACKNOWLEDGMENTS

Writing and publishing a book is far more complex than I ever imagined. I am indebted to many people who have enabled me to complete this book.

First, I have to thank my special friend, Patty Clements, for your kind critiques of my podcasts and manuscripts as well as your positive outlook. Thank you, too, for proofreading my book!

Second, I have to thank my daughter, Laura Jordan for her enthusiasm and creative ideas for my books and Ministry. I especially thank you for all of your help in the social media world.

Third, thank you to my "coaches":
- My long-time friend and fellow "Patriot Pastor" Dan Fisher, for encouraging me in my God-N-America Ministry and in writing and publishing my books.

- My friend of many years, Waymon Hinson, who encouraged me to take on the tasks of my God-N-America Ministry and coached me in the rough patches.

- Lana Wooldridge for proofreading the book and making my final corrections.

- My writing instructor, Andrea Foster, for broadening my horizons in the writing world.

I really could go on and on thanking people for their contributions to this book and my life. I like being an author and I hope to write more books and blogs. Be sure to check out GodNAmerica.com for podcasts, blogs, and more.

Introduction

Someone has said that a sermon does not have to be eternal to be immortal. I agree. I know that the more a preacher learns, the more he wants to share. Sometimes the sermons are more prolonged than people need. I believe, in general, that the adage "less is more" is true.

I have tried to learn and apply that lesson. I am sure there were times that Jesus spoke to His hearers for a long time. **John 13-17** may have been one of those times. There is MUCH information in those chapters about the last night of His life. However, we also see that He kept His comments to a minimum on many occasions. Just look at the brevity of the Sermon on the Mount (**Matthew 5-7**) and its impact. He left His audience amazed at His words as He spoke with authority. Often briefer is better.

The goal of this book is to say a lot in a little. I prefer to plumb the depths of a little rather than wade in the shallows of a lot. In fact, as a nineteen-year-old, the very first book of the Bible I read was the book of Proverbs. It contains significant truths in a few words.

Brevity with purpose is the power of the devotional. Through a few words in a few minutes, we can gain great insights. These insights can stay with us all day.

The Preacher declared in **Ecclesiastes 4:12** (NKJV), ". . . a threefold cord is not quickly broken." My goals for this book are threefold. I intend to teach scripture, retell American history, and make contemporary applications in the lessons.

Sometimes, the lessons are obvious. Sometimes the lessons are more obscure. I believe that we can see the truths of God's word played out in the lives of some of our American heroes as well as in the lives of biblical characters. As a result, we also want to apply those biblical principles to our lives.

We might express those biblical principles in the form of deliberately standing against tyranny. We may express them by bringing justice to the disadvantaged. We might even express them by defending the helpless. All of our valued actions stem from a firm reliance on the One who has given us "everything that pertains to life and godliness" (**2 Peter 1:3**).

This book is a collection of manuscripts from my devotional podcasts at **GodNAmerica.com**. In each of these, I encourage us to *"Keep The Light Burning!"*

The light was an early element of all that God created, "*in the beginning*." The light predates the creation of the sun and moon (see **Genesis 1:3; 14-19**). The light was, and is, important to God as it overcomes darkness and brings order.

Light can be a metaphor for illumination. That illumination can be mental understanding or spiritual enhancement. We can even gain insights into wisdom and call it illumination. Whatever the case, we can "see the light."

The Spirit of God enables us to see the light in our darkness. In fact, without His aid, we will miss His message. Charles Spurgeon, the nineteenth-century "Prince of Preachers," elaborated on Jesus' declaration regarding the Holy Spirit in **John 16:8** (NKJV): "*8 And when He has come, He will convict the world of sin, and of righteousness, and of judgment.*" Notice Spurgeon's comment:

> . . . You will find that all your affection and your tears and your earnest description of the love of Jesus will be powerless against human hearts, unless the eternal Spirit shall drive home your appeals.[1]

When God reveals the light of His truth, we investigate and incorporate it. As a logical follow-up, we share it. Thus, we "*Keep The Light Burning!*"

I hope that this book informs a little and inspires a lot. Seeing others take God at His word and put it into practice stimulates us. There is something motivational about seeing people obey God despite their fears and challenges. Our biblical heroes and vital American figures were people just like we are. We can follow their examples in taking God at His word. If they did it, we can, too!

---

[1] Carter, Tom, editor. *Spurgeon at His Best*. Grand Rapids, Michigan, Baker Book House, 1988, p. 304.

Chapter 1: Keep The Light Burning!

Psalm 119:105 (NKJV)
> Your word is a lamp to my feet
> And a light to my path.

The sea enthralls me. My father was a career enlisted man of twenty-four years in the U.S. Navy, and so, we generally lived by the ocean while I was growing up. As a result, I am captivated by the beach, the breeze, and the breakers.

Along with the allure of the sea, lighthouses have enchanted me. I have studied their purpose and history. Over the years, lighthouses have stood vigil by the ocean, giving direction, location, and safety to the ships as they come and go. In the bygone eras, lighthouse keepers were indispensable to the safety of seagoing vessels. Sometimes they and their families were the only assistance some sailors would have in storm-tossed seas.

In the mid-nineteenth century, Abbie Burgess performed a remarkable feat as the young daughter of a lighthouse keeper named Samuel Burgess. He tended the twin lighthouse towers at the Matinicus Rock Lighthouse, Maine.

In January of 1856, Mrs. Burgess, who had a disability, was ill, so Mr. Burgess decided to go ashore for medicine and other needed supplies. To go, he had to entrust his oldest daughter, Abbie, with the critical role of keeping the lighthouses in his absence. As he pushed away in his rowboat, and he said to her, "Keep the lights burning, Abbie."

Lighthouse keeping was no easy task on good days. The keepers had to maintain the lights in every way. The keeper had to carry heavy buckets of oil up the stairs to burn in the lights. For Abbie, not only was there work in the lighthouse, but she also had to take care of her family and the animals on their island. But it got even more difficult.

While her father was away, a storm rushed in from the sea. Abbie's father could not return to his post with his family on the island for about four weeks. Supplies on the island ran dangerously low. Abbie's mother drifted in and out of consciousness as the storm raged. Their living quarters flooded, and the family had to seek higher ground. They then moved into one of the lighthouse towers.

Yet, all through the storm, day and night, the lighthouses' beams could be seen. If the storm caught any ship, the lighthouses would warn them of the dangerous rocks and reefs. For those weeks, Abbie kept the lights burning!

I am impressed with the grit of that sixteen-year-old girl and her commitment to the task before her. That ultimately leads me to Jesus and the task before Him. He passed His task to us.

Jesus is THE light of the world (**John 8:12**). He directs us in safety. His "beam" is an unmistakable pattern and message of love and acceptance. After his death, burial, and resurrection, Jesus gave His disciples their marching orders to finish carrying out His mission. We call this the "Great Commission." We make disciples throughout the world (**Matthew 28:18-20**). In so doing, we are to be the light of the world (**Matthew 5:14**) and "Keep the Light Burning" in our age to keep His message fresh and new.

I borrowed "*Keep The Light Burning!*" as my signature for emails and letters. The phrase reminds me of the light of Jesus in our world of darkness. Even a tiny amount of light is more powerful than darkness. Yet, it is up to us to keep that light burning so light can overcome darkness. It is necessary so men may know the truth and be free (**John 8:31-32**).

John 1:5 (NKJV) reads:
   ⁵And the light shines in the darkness, and the darkness did not comprehend it.

Darkness can be powerful and frightening. If you are afraid of the dark, "Keep The Light Burning!" Light is more powerful. The psalmist points out in **Psalm 27:1** (NKJV):

The Lord is my light and my salvation;
Whom shall I fear?

We have the light of God in many forms:
- The Light of God's Word in your life
- The Light of God's Word in the world
- The light of genuine knowledge of God
- The light of the true history of America by telling His story in our history
- The Light of Liberty that only comes from God

Let's Keep The Light *of God Burning* in its many forms!

Personal Action Pages

Pray Through 1 John 1:5-7 (NKJV)

[5] This is the message which we have heard from Him and declare to you, that God is light and in Him is no darkness at all. [6] If we say that we have fellowship with Him, and walk in darkness, we lie and do not practice the truth. [7] But if we walk in the light as He is in the light, we have fellowship with one another, and the blood of Jesus Christ His Son cleanses us from all sin.

Ponder:

1. How has God been light to your life?
2. How do you "walk in the light?"
3. When you are afraid, how does the light of God give you comfort?
4. How have you been the "light of the world" to others?

Practice:

I will keep the light of God burning today by:

Personal Observations

Chapter 2: Telling His Story in Our History

Psalm 33:12 (NKJV)

Blessed is the nation whose God is the Lord,
The people He has chosen as His own inheritance.

The mission of God-N-America is to "reconnect God and America by telling His story in our history." You see, whether intentionally or by apathy, we have forgotten our history. America has had a glorious past. That past was not just about conquest and victory in times of conflict; it was about allegiance to God, unequaled in modern times.

This idea captivated me a few years ago when I heard some recorded sermons by one of my favorite preachers, Bob Russell of Louisville, Kentucky. In those lessons, he emphasized America's early connections to God and the Providence of God in our history. Three stories captured my attention.

First, there was the story of George Washington at the Battle of Monongahela during the French and Indian War in 1755. Washington was a colonial officer under British General Braddock. The British and Americans lost the battle that day, but George Washington seemed miraculously protected. Years later, an Indian chief who had fought against him said of Washington that he was "the man who is the particular favorite of heaven, who could never die in battle."

Second, there is the story of the Continental Army that was trapped by the British at Brooklyn Heights on Long Island on August 27, 1776. Washington evacuated his troops all night to escape the British. However, by morning a great number of soldiers remained on the island. They would have undoubtedly have been killed or captured by the British had it not been for the peculiar fog that encompassed both armies. The providential fog enabled Washington to remove those troops. Those who were there called it Divine Providence.

Third, there is the story of the Battle of Yorktown, in 1781. Some historians refer to it as the "Miraculous Convergence." A providential storm prevented the British from escaping the American Continental Army. It brought the American War for Independence to an end.

As I investigated our history further, I found many more stories of what appears to be divine intervention in the establishment of our nation. My examination showed some fantastic things about our Founders and Framers. These men were not a collection of atheists, agnostics, and deists, as some have led us to believe. For the most part, these men were devout Christians. They had a biblical worldview in which they based their actions on the Holy Scriptures more than the philosophies of men.

America was not a chosen nation like Israel. America was more of a "choosing nation." Our ancestors chose to follow God and uphold the teachings of Jesus. Many who came to America did not come for "gold" but God. Like the Pilgrims, they came to "advance Christian faith," meaning they were to be missionaries to the natives in the New World, not their conquerors or masters.

Their Bible study revealed God's will in every part of life, from the individual to the family to the community to the nation. They chose to incorporate biblical principles into their lives and then into the life of our nation. The results of their faith-filled labors remind me of God's affirmation of non-Jews who embrace Him in **Isaiah 56:6-8** (NKJV)

> [6] "Also the sons of the foreigner
> Who join themselves to the Lord, to serve Him,

And to love the name of the Lord, to be His
servants—
Everyone who keeps from defiling the Sabbath,
And holds fast My covenant—
[7] Even them I will bring to My holy mountain,
And make them joyful in My house of prayer.
Their burnt offerings and their sacrifices
Will be accepted on My altar;
For My house shall be called a house of prayer for
all nations."
[8] The Lord God, who gathers the outcasts of Israel,
says,
"Yet I will gather to him
Others besides those who are gathered to him."

I believe God has a special place in His heart for those who choose to follow Him. Someone has said that God does not have any "grandchildren." Every person who follows God is His son or daughter. It is incumbent upon every generation to develop a personal, deep-seated relationship with God. That is, every person of every generation has the opportunity for a fresh approach to Him.

Even the chosen nation of Israel had the opportunity to know God anew in each generation. Yet, their personal and national relationships with Him often ebbed and flowed. America has, too, and God called us back to Him through events like the Great Awakenings.

The writer of Proverbs stated in **Proverbs 1:7** (NKJV):

> The fear of the Lord is the beginning of knowledge, But fools despise wisdom and instruction.

Our awe and reverence for God is the beginning point of all knowledge. It is foolish to neglect Him. It is foolish to neglect His story in our history.

Jesus said:

> "I am the way, the truth, and the life. No one comes to the Father except through Me. [7] "If you had known Me, you would have known My Father also; and from now on you know Him and have seen Him." (**John 14:6-7**, NKJV).

Just as our forefathers chanted to the British, "We have no king but King Jesus," we can declare His authority for our lives as our Lord, King, and Savior.

Keep The Light *of Telling His Story in Our History* Burning!

Personal Action Pages

Pray Through Isaiah 56:6-8 (NKJV)

⁶ "Also the sons of the foreigner
Who join themselves to the Lord, to serve Him,
And to love the name of the Lord, to be His servants—
Everyone who keeps from defiling the Sabbath,
And holds fast My covenant—
⁷ Even them I will bring to My holy mountain,
And make them joyful in My house of prayer.
Their burnt offerings and their sacrifices
Will be accepted on My altar;
For My house shall be called a house of prayer for all nations."
⁸ The Lord God, who gathers the outcasts of Israel, says,
"Yet I will gather to him
Others besides those who are gathered to him."

Ponder

What impresses you about the hand of God in peoples' lives in scripture?

How have you seen God at work in our world?

What American characters have expressed active faith in their lives?

Have you seen yourself as a "child of God" or as a "grandchild"?

Practice

Today I will tell His story in our history by:

Personal Observations

Chapter 3: On Edge at the Edge

Exodus 14:10-14 (NKJV)

[10] And when Pharaoh drew near, the children of Israel lifted their eyes, and behold, the Egyptians marched after them. So they were very afraid, and the children of Israel cried out to the Lord. [11] Then they said to Moses, "Because there were no graves in Egypt, have you taken us away to die in the wilderness? Why have you so dealt with us, to bring us up out of Egypt? [12] Is this not the word that we told you in Egypt, saying, 'Let us alone that we may serve the Egyptians'? For it would have been better for us to serve the Egyptians than that we should die in the wilderness."

[13] And Moses said to the people, "Do not be afraid. Stand still, and see the salvation of the Lord, which He will accomplish for you today. For the Egyptians whom you see today, you shall see again no more forever. [14] The Lord will fight for you, and you shall hold your peace."

The Hebrews escaped Egyptian slavery by the power of God and His leadership through Moses. They found themselves at the Red Sea. Suddenly, Pharaoh's army approached, and the people feared for their lives. However, right at the edge of destruction, God rescued them. That same God is at work today.

Maybe you are a bit like me. You have looked around and have observed that America is in deep trouble. The flood of ungodly Marxist philosophy is advancing in every area of our culture. Americans cannot stem the tide because we left the anchor of our souls and the soul of our nation. That anchor is our God and His scriptures.

We are drifting over the deadly waterfalls of neglect. I have heard some say that no country in history that reached the same level of depravity as ours has ever made a comeback. Instead, those nations ceased to exist or have become irrelevant. It seems we are indeed at a precarious moment in our history.

Does it make your heart sick? Do we realize that we are on the brink of losing everything for which our forefathers sacrificed? All because we have been too busy, too preoccupied, and too distracted to embrace God fully.

I realize that you probably are a fully committed follower

of Jesus. But, in 2021, George Barna found that about 9% of Christians live out a truly biblical worldview. The 91% are really "Christian in Name Only."[2]

The majority of Christians today are much like the Jews Jesus referred to in **Mark 7:6-7** when he quoted **Isaiah 29:13** (NKJV):

> Therefore the Lord said: "Inasmuch as these people draw near with their mouths
> And honor Me with their lips,
> But have removed their hearts far from Me,
> And their fear toward Me is taught by the commandment of men,

Somehow, you have been able to rise above the distractions and focus on God with all of your heart, soul, and might. But for the most part, we have created a spiritual vacuum in the nation among our leaders.

Have you noticed the importance of leadership in scripture? When the people had godly leaders, they were godly. When they had ungodly leaders, the people were

---

[2] Shepherd, Josh. "Survey Finds Only 9% of Self-Identified Christians Hold to Biblical Worldview." *The Roys Report*, edited by Julie Roys, The Roys Report, 10 Sept. 2021, julieroys.com/george-barna-survey-biblical-worldview/

ungodly. You see this in the books of Judges, 1 and 2 Samuel, 1 and 2 Kings, and 1 and 2 Chronicles.

Many of our early political leaders were men of faith. They took God and His word seriously. They were not seeking power as much as they were submitting to the God of Israel.

- George Washington led Congress to worship at his inauguration in New York City.
- Thomas Jefferson attended worship services at a church in the Capitol building every Sunday, setting the pace and giving an example for the nation to follow.
- Andrew Jackson made this declaration: "The Bible is the rock on which our Republic rests."
- In more modern times, Dwight Eisenhower led prayer at his inauguration in January 1953.

We may complain about and criticize our political leaders. We may be right in our observation, but we are the root of the problem. When James Garfield was a congressman, he made an astute observation:

"Now more than ever before, the people are responsible for the character of their Congress. If that body be ignorant, reckless, and corrupt, it is because the people tolerate ignorance, recklessness and corruption."

Charles Finney was a leading evangelist during the Second Great Awakening. He went even further to the root of the problem as he addressed his fellow preachers:

"Brethren, our preaching will bear its legitimate fruits. If immorality prevails in the land, the fault is ours in a great degree. If there is a decay of conscience, the pulpit is responsible for it. If the public press lacks moral discrimination, the pulpit is responsible for it. If the church is degenerate and worldly, the pulpit is responsible for it. If the world loses its interest in religion, the pulpit is responsible for it. If Satan rules in our halls of legislation, the pulpit is responsible for it. If our politics become so corrupt that the very foundations of our government are ready to fall away, the pulpit is responsible for it. Let us not ignore this fact, my dear brethren; but let us lay it to heart, and be thoroughly awake to our responsibility in respect to the morals of this nation." ~ Charles Finney, "The Decay of Conscience," New York, December 4, 1873.

Christians have bought into the devil's lie that Bible-believing people should separate from government. So, preachers have stopped preaching civic responsibility. Christians have agreeably abdicated their duty concerning their country. They have then become so "heavenly-minded that they are of no earthly good."

The question for us: Is it too late to fix the problem? Moses led the Hebrews to the Red Sea, and God opened it for them. Pharaoh's army drowned in the sea when they tried to follow the Hebrews. Maybe God will rescue us at just the right moment as well. **Galatians 4:4-5** (NKJV) reminds us of God's timing:

> [4] But when the fullness of the time had come, God sent forth His Son, born of a woman, born under the law, [5] To redeem those who were under the law, that we might receive the adoption as sons.

It is likely beyond our ability to fix our problems. **Psalm 121:1-2** (NKJV) read:

> [1] I will lift up my eyes to the hills—
> From whence comes my help?
> [2] My help comes from the Lord,
> Who made heaven and earth.

Let us all commit ourselves to the LORD entirely and follow Him willfully. HE is our hope. HE is our salvation. HE leads us here and home.

Keep The Light *of Godly Leadership* Burning!

Personal Action Pages

Pray Through Psalm 121:1-2 (NKJV):

[1] I will lift up my eyes to the hills—
From whence comes my help?
[2] My help comes from the Lord,
Who made heaven and earth.

Ponder

1. How do you feel when your world begins to fall apart? Where do you turn?
2. Where have you seen people draw near to God merely with "lip service"?
3. What it is your obligation to America as a believer?
4. How is your civic duty also a spiritual one?
5. In what ways is this a matter of God's timing?

Practice

Make a list of civic groups or causes in which you can be involved.

In addition to prayer, today I will serve our nation by:

Personal Observations

Personal Observations

Chapter 4: Letting Liberty Ring

Romans 15:4 (NKJV)

4 For whatever things were written before were written for our learning, that we through the patience and comfort of the Scriptures might have hope.

Psalm 78:1-4 (NKJV)

Give ear, O my people, to my law;
Incline your ears to the words of my mouth.
2 I will open my mouth in a parable;
I will utter dark sayings of old,
3 Which we have heard and known,
And our fathers have told us.
4 We will not hide them from their children,
Telling to the generation to come the praises of the Lord,
And His strength and His wonderful works that He has done.

We see a crucial principle in scripture of knowing our past. The things written in scripture are for our benefit. God's words inform us how people of the past lived before God and the consequences of their actions. In scripture, story after story gives us examples of what God can do through people.

As one preacher said, "If it's in the Word, it should be in the world." So we read scripture and try to activate what God declared in our time.

Recently (2022), Florida governor Ron DeSantis said:

> "People need to be taught why America was founded, what the principles that made our country unique were. They need to be taught that our rights do not come from government; they come from God."

That principle of knowing history applies to America's history, too. The early Founders were Christian people seeking God and establishing His principles in every aspect of life. Over the years, we have forgotten many stories of our Founders. Likewise, we have forgotten the providential hand of God.

I want to explore a little of what it cost our founding generation to secure our liberty. The pledge of the signers at the end of the Declaration of Independence reads:

> "And for the support of this Declaration, with a firm

reliance on the protection of divine Providence, we mutually pledge to each other our Lives, our Fortunes, and our sacred Honor."

Of the fifty-six men who signed the Declaration of Independence, nine died of wounds or hardships during the war. Five were captured, imprisoned, and tortured. Several of them lost their wives, children, or entire families. Two wives were brutalized and tortured. All were the victims of manhunts and driven from their homes by British soldiers at one time or another. Twelve signers had their homes completely burned. Seventeen lost everything they owned. Here are a few examples:

- Carter Braxton was a wealthy planter and merchant. He saw the British Navy sweep his ships from the seas. He sold his home and properties to pay his debts and died in poverty.
- The British pursued Thomas McKean. He was forced to move his family continuously. He served in Congress without pay, keeping his family in hiding. The British seized his possessions, and he died in poverty.
- At the Battle of Yorktown, Thomas Nelson Jr. noted that British General Cornwallis used his home for his headquarters. General George Washington refused to fire on the dwelling out of respect to Nelson. Nelson privately urged Washington to open

fire on his home, saying it was no longer his home but was now the enemy's headquarters. The Continental Army subsequently destroyed his home. Nelson died in poverty.

- Frances Lewis had his home and properties destroyed by the British. They jailed his wife, and she died within a few months.

- John Hart was driven from his wife's bedside as she was dying. Their thirteen children fled for their lives as the British laid waste his fields and his gristmill. He lived in forests and caves for more than a year, returning home to find his wife dead and all of his children missing. He never saw them again.

How easily some of us would give up our liberty! Our forefathers paid a great price and sometimes the ultimate price. I know of preachers, church leaders, and Christians who would instead give up what those Christians brought us rather than stand up for it. Our silence is approval for the evil and tyranny overtaking our country. What will history say about us?

Keep The Light *of Liberty* Burning!

Personal Action Pages

Pray Through Psalm 78:1-4 (NKJV)

Give ear, O my people, to my law;
Incline your ears to the words of my mouth.
^{2} I will open my mouth in a parable;
I will utter dark sayings of old,
^{3} Which we have heard and known,
And our fathers have told us.
^{4} We will not hide them from their children,
Telling to the generation to come the praises of the
Lord,
And His strength and His wonderful works that He has
done.

Ponder

1. In what ways does knowing our past establish our future?
2. Why would evil men want to erase our national history? Our biblical history?
3. In what ways does grace not equal "ease?"
4. Why do you think our Christian Founders had such a strong desire for national liberty? How are faith and liberty connected?
5. What lessons of history, both American and biblical, are you passing on? Why?

Practice

Take time to reflect on your prayers and their answers. What has God done for you? What has God done through you?

Make a list of the sacrifices you are willing to make for liberty.

Personal Observations

Chapter 5: The Grand Old Flag (Flag Day)

When I was young, I had some real patriots as teachers. That wasn't unusual then, and I appreciate their God-based love for America. One year my elementary school class learned the lyrics to many patriotic songs. One of these was "You're a Grand Old Flag."

George M. Cohan wrote "You're a Grand Old Flag" for his 1906 stage musical *George Washington, Jr.* The musical introduced the song to the public in the play's first act on opening night, February 6, 1906, in New York's Herald Square Theater. It was the first song from a musical to sell over a million copies of sheet music.

The original lyrics for this perpetual George M. Cohan favorite came, as Cohan later explained, from an encounter he had with a Civil War veteran of Gettysburg. Cohan noticed the vet held a carefully folded but ragged old flag. The man reportedly then turned to Cohan and said, "She's a grand old rag." Cohan thought it was a great line. He originally named his tune "You're a Grand Old Rag." So many objected to calling the flag a "rag," however, that he "gave 'em what they wanted" and switched words to "You're a Grand Old Flag." Here is the chorus:[3]

> You're a grand old flag
> You're a high-flying flag
> And forever in peace may you wave
> You're the emblem of
> The land I love
> The home of the free and the brave
> Ev'ry heart beats true
> Under the red, white, and blue
> Where there's never a boast or a brag
> But should old acquaintance be forgot
> Keep your eye on the grand old flag

Maybe you saw James Cagney sing it in the movie "*Yankee Doodle Dandy*." He said it was his favorite movie of the sixty or so in which he starred. Cagney made the movie at the beginning of WWII, filled with flag-waving patriotism.

"Flag Day," according to William Federer, June 14, 1777, was when the Continental Congress selected our flag of

---

[3] *You're a Grand Old Flag*. Library of Congress, Washington, DC, 2002. Web.. Retrieved from the Library of Congress, <www.loc.gov/item/ihas.200000026.

thirteen stars and thirteen stripes.[4] In 1916, President Woodrow Wilson signed the proclamation making June 14 "Flag Day." President Eisenhower officially added "One Nation Under God" to the pledge of allegiance on Flag Day, June 14, 1954. He stated that it reaffirmed the transcendence of faith in America's heritage.

In other words, the flag is about "*GodNAmerica!*" When we delve into the history of America, we can see the flag as a symbol of the nation. Each star represents each state in our Union. Each stripe represents the original thirteen colonies. As we added states to our Union, Congress initially intended to add a stripe and a star. The flag for the war of 1812 had fifteen stars and stripes. That proved too cumbersome, so we retained the original thirteen stripes and added stars to represent the states.

But the flag is more than a representation of the country. It is a reminder of the heritage of the nation. We established our early colonies on the biblical principles of the "*Laws of Nature and Nature's God.*" He is the Giver of our unalienable rights of life, liberty, and property. In 1787, as Congress was fighting over the establishment of

---

[4] Federer, William J. *American Minute*. St. Louis, Amerisearch, Inc., 2012, p. 172.

the Constitution, Benjamin Franklin offered a God-based solution to the problem. He stated:

> "We have been assured, Sir, in the Sacred Writings, that "except the Lord build the House, they labor in vain that build it." I firmly believe this; and I also believe that without his concurring aid we shall succeed in this political building no better than the Builders of Babel . . ." He went on to call for a time of prayer in regard to the work at hand. Soon, almost miraculously, the Constitution was written and affirmed.

So, especially honor the flag. As God-fearing patriots, let's honor it every day by remembering our history and heritage. We truly were established as "one nation under God, indivisible, with liberty and justice for all."

Psalm 33:12 (ESV)

> Blessed is the nation whose God is the Lord,
> the people whom he has chosen as his heritage!
> Honor our flag as a way to tell His story in our history.

Keep The Light *of Our Godly Heritage* Burning!

Personal Action Pages

Pray Through Psalm 33:10-17

[10] The Lord brings the counsel of the nations to nothing;
He makes the plans of the peoples of no effect.
[11] The counsel of the Lord stands forever,
The plans of His heart to all generations.
[12] Blessed is the nation whose God is the Lord,
The people He has chosen as His own inheritance.
[13] The Lord looks from heaven;
He sees all the sons of men. [14] From the place of His dwelling He looks
On all the inhabitants of the earth;
[15] He fashions their hearts individually;
He considers all their works.
[16] No king is saved by the multitude of an army;
A mighty man is not delivered by great strength.
[17] A horse is a vain hope for safety;
Neither shall it deliver any by its great strength.

Ponder

The story of our first flags.

The significance of the Stars; Stripes; and their Colors.

How the American flag can symbolize Christians and Christian values.

Practice

For Flag Day or a study of the flag I will display the American flag if possible.

Personal Observations

Chapter 6: Liberty for All

1 Peter 2:16 (NKJV)

[16] as free, yet not using liberty as a cloak for vice, but as bondservants of God.

Senate Chaplain Peter Marshall once described freedom in this manner:

May we think of freedom, not as the right to do as we please, but as the opportunity to do what is right.

We realize by observation and revelation that we get into trouble when we let ourselves be our guides. We've watched as many significant cities fell under the dominion of rioters and wondered why mayors and governors wouldn't defend their constituents. We read in scripture of the moral depravity of self-direction – even of Israel when according to **Judges 21:25** (NKJV):

[25] In those days *there was* no king in Israel; everyone did *what was* right in his own eyes.

The freedom or liberty that God gives us is not to see how

immoral or raucous we can become. Instead, it is to help us become all that God made us to be. That freedom is from inside, out.

You see, God created us initially to be free. Before sin entered the world, mankind was to have dominion over everything on earth according to **Genesis 1:28**. That's freedom. Everything would obey Adam as is seen in Jesus' ministry (as He is the last Adam, according to **1 Corinthians 15:45**).

Do you remember some of His miracles over nature? He changed water to wine instantly (nature does that slowly as rain falls to the ground, the roots of the vine absorb it and then gives it to the grape; but Jesus did it instantly). He healed the sick. Our immune systems can heal some diseases, but Jesus healed instantly. He stopped the wind and waves on the Sea of Galilee with a simple command. He gave catches of fish to fishers like Peter.

Even though God made us free, we allowed sin into the camp. We became entangled in its destruction.

In a "Turning Point" devotional by David Jeremiah, he

described the danger of sinful entanglements.[5] He wrote:

During the Christmas season of 2020, a man dressed in a Santa outfit was paragliding over Sacramento, tossing down candy canes to children. He wanted to spread Christmas cheer. Unfortunately, he sailed too low and became entangled in power lines. He wasn't hurt, but the children didn't know what to think of Santa dangling and helpless. Firefighters were able to rescue the man.

According to **Isaiah 40:31**, those who wait upon the Lord "shall mount up with wings like eagles." But Jesus warned against becoming entangled with "the cares of this world and the deceitfulness of riches" (**Matthew 13:22**). It's easy for us to become entangled in the high voltage lines of worldly cares at just the moment we should be soaring by faith.

God made us wonderfully in order to fulfill His purpose. Keep your eyes on Him, wait on the Lord, mount up daily on the winds of His grace, and be aware of anything that will entangle your flight.

The apostle Peter made this observation in **2 Peter 2:20** (NLT):

---

[5] Jeremiah, David. "Tangled Up." *Turning Point*, edited by David Jeremiah, Turning Point, 6 July 2021, TurningPoint@davidjeremiah.org.

And when people escape from the wickedness of the world by knowing our Lord and Savior Jesus Christ and then get tangled up and enslaved by sin again, they are worse off than before.

God made us as free people. Free from the domination and control of sin – both inside and out. We can only have that when we are devoted to Him. As a prisoner, the apostle Paul preached to Agrippa. In **Acts 26:29** (NKJV) he declared:

> [29] And Paul said, "I would to God that not only you, but also all who hear me today, might become both almost and altogether such as I am, except for these chains."

Paul's freedom was an inside-out proposition. In Christ his spirit was free, regardless of what happened externally. That's where it begins for all of us.

Albert Camus stated:

> The only way to deal with an unfree world is to become so absolutely free that your very existence is an act of rebellion.

No wonder Christians have been persecuted throughout

history. They have had freedom!

Keep The Light *of Your Freedom* Burning!

Personal Action Pages

Pray Through

1 Peter 2:13-17 (NKJV)

[13] Therefore submit yourselves to every ordinance of man for the Lord's sake, whether to the king as supreme, [14] or to governors, as to those who are sent by him for the punishment of evildoers and *for the* praise of those who do good. [15] For this is the will of God, that by doing good you may put to silence the ignorance of foolish men— [16] as free, yet not using liberty as a cloak for vice, but as bondservants of God. [17] Honor all *people.* Love the brotherhood. Fear God. Honor the king.

Ponder

1. How much do we submit to governments? Is submission unlimited or are there limits?
2. How is freedom an "inside-out" proposition?
3. What specific things corrupt our freedom?
4. How can freedom be an act of rebellion? How is that especially true for Christians?

Practice

Today I will respectfully exercise my God-given freedom of _________________ .

Personal Observations

48

Chapter 7: Why Liberty?

"Liberty" is a sweet word to the true American. Today we are talking a lot about "liberty." There is a panic at the thought of losing our freedoms and unalienable rights. But why is that?

Along with "liberty," we've been hearing an increased emphasis on patriotism. There are more and more "patriotic events." More and more companies are promoting patriotism, at least in their names and products. There are even more and more churches rising with the tide of patriotism. But why is that?

Today could be one of those times that people are just cashing in on a current trend. Patriotism is selling among the majority of Americans right now. Companies are making money by waving the flag and calling themselves patriots. But is this why we seek liberty?

We may not be interested in cashing in on the current dilemma. Still, we may need to examine our motives for liberty. We may be seeking liberty for our convenience and ease. If we lose our liberty, we will have hardships. Communist countries don't have plenty, they have a shortage. They have a low view of human life. Loss of liberty is indeed an inconvenience, but is that all we care about?

There is more to liberty than convenience. Liberty or freedom is ultimately about the person and presence of God. Consider the following verses:

- **2 Corinthians 3:17** (NKJV): [17] Now the Lord is the Spirit; and where the Spirit of the Lord *is*, there *is* liberty.

- **2 Peter 2:19** (NKJV): [19] While they promise them liberty, they themselves are slaves of corruption; for by whom a person is overcome, by him also he is brought into bondage.

- **Galatians 5:1** (NKJV): Stand fast therefore in the liberty by which Christ has made us free, and do not be entangled again with a yoke of bondage.

God wants us to have liberty, both personally and nationally. We can have personal freedom internally regardless of the externals. That kind of freedom comes only with the presence of the Spirit of God in our lives.

We can't have it apart from Him. We can't have Him apart from faith-filled lives. With God, we can have both internal and external liberty.

Our Founding Fathers understood that knowing God is freedom. This is why they dedicated the nation they created to God. He is the author of liberty and justice for all.

How important is liberty to a true American? George Washington purportedly said:

"I'll die on my feet before I'll live on my knees!"

Patrick Henry declared:

"Is life so dear, or peace so sweet, as to be purchased at the price of chains and slavery? Forbid it, Almighty God! I know not what course others may take, but as for me, give me Liberty or give me death!"

Some Americans today would carelessly throw away the liberty God provided for us through the sacrifice of patriots. Maybe that is because we have not paid the price for liberty. Maybe it is because we take it for granted that we will always have liberty and lose the vigilance to keep it.

We miss most what we lose. We appreciate most the things for which we sacrifice.

Zephaniah 1:12 (NKJV) fits our contemporary culture.

> 12 "And it shall come to pass at that time
> *That* I will search Jerusalem with lamps,
> And punish the men
> Who are settled in complacency,
> Who say in their heart,
> 'The LORD will not do good,
> Nor will He do evil.'

God's people lost their liberty out of complacency. Liberty lost is a lesson for us.

Holding our liberty means we are good stewards of a special gift from God. It means living out what God has placed within. Don't give up any Liberty God has given!

Keep The Light *of Sweet Liberty* Burning!

Personal Action Pages

Pray Through Zephaniah 1:12-18 (NKJV)

[12] "And it shall come to pass at that time
That I will search Jerusalem with lamps,
And punish the men
Who are settled in complacency,
Who say in their heart,
'The LORD will not do good,
Nor will He do evil.'

[13] Therefore their goods shall become booty,
And their houses a desolation;
They shall build houses, but not inhabit *them;*
They shall plant vineyards, but not drink their wine."

[14] The great day of the LORD *is* near;
It is near and hastens quickly.
The noise of the day of the LORD is bitter;
There the mighty men shall cry out.
[15] That day *is* a day of wrath,
A day of trouble and distress,
A day of devastation and desolation,
A day of darkness and gloominess,
A day of clouds and thick darkness,
[16] A day of trumpet and alarm

Against the fortified cities

And against the high towers.

[17] "I will bring distress upon men,
And they shall walk like blind men,
Because they have sinned against the LORD;
Their blood shall be poured out like dust,
And their flesh like refuse."

[18] Neither their silver nor their gold
Shall be able to deliver them
In the day of the LORD's wrath;
But the whole land shall be devoured
By the fire of His jealousy,
For He will make speedy riddance
Of all those who dwell in the land.

Ponder

1. Why do we panic over the thought of losing our liberty?
2. How serious is it to lose our liberty?
3. Why are some willingly giving up their liberty?
4. How does God want us to use our liberty?
5. In what ways is liberty a gift for our stewardship?

Practice

I will hold my liberty by _______________________.

Personal Observations

Chapter 8: God Shed His Grace on Thee

2 Corinthians 9:8 (NKJV)

[8] And God *is* able to make all grace abound toward you, that you, always having all sufficiency in all *things,* may have an abundance for every good work.

I am sure you've been hearing all of the rhetoric regarding how bad America is. Athletes who represent us on the athletic field turn their backs on the national anthem and kneel out of disrespect. It's too bad they can't find another country they can be proud of and represent.

The truth is, America is a flawed country because flawed people compose it. We were a flawed nation from the beginning. It is true today. The men who signed the Declaration of Independence admitted their frailty. They were also determined to live so that God would direct their steps. Many of them claimed to see the providential hand of God as we made our break with Great Britain. It has been seen repeatedly through the years.

Today, a cultural revolution is trying to distance us from

our biblical heritage. "One nation under God" was what our ancestors foresaw. Today, God is drummed out of our schools, courthouses, and political parties, either formally or informally. We are taking on a godless political mindset instead of a godly one.

John Adams said it best:

> "Our Constitution was made only for a moral and religious people. It is wholly inadequate to the government of any other."[6]

So, why has America prospered if we have been such an inadequate people? It isn't because we are without sin. It isn't because all of our works have been so noble. Maybe it has to do with grace. **Ephesians 2:8-10** (ESV) reminds us:

> [8] For by grace you have been saved through faith. And this is not your own doing; it is the gift of God, [9] not a result of works, so that no one may boast. [10] For we are his workmanship, created in Christ Jesus for good works, which God prepared beforehand, that we should

---

[6] Federer, William J. *American Quotations.* Amerisearch, Inc., 2013, p. 661.

walk in them.

God can save us from many things. He can save us from evil, danger, disease, addictions, and sin itself. We generally think of grace and eternal salvation, but it can mean more. America truly was saved from the dangerous tyranny of King George in the late eighteenth century – by grace.

We didn't deserve that salvation, but God gave it. Many Americans back then believed He orchestrated it in His sovereignty. Maybe so, but as I have said before, Israel was God's "chosen nation," and America became the "choosing nation" of God. He has done great things through both nations.

The prophet relates this idea in **Isaiah 56:3** (ESV):

> [3] Let not the foreigner who has joined himself to the LORD say,
>   "The LORD will surely separate me from his people";

And again in **verse 8:**

[8] The Lord GOD,
   who gathers the outcasts of Israel, declares,
"I will gather yet others to him
   besides those already gathered."

Americans chose to follow God and put His word into practice in their lives. So, America prospered as she followed and struggled when she didn't. Where would you say we are today in our relationship with God? Maybe we are still standing, though teetering, because of God's grace.

In the words of the song, "America the Beautiful," – "God shed His grace on thee; and crowned thy good with brotherhood, from sea to shining sea." But, don't forget, the song also says of America – "God mend thine every flaw, Confirm thy soul in self-control, Thy liberty in law!" That's an appeal to His grace!

I am going to close with this July 4 tweet from former boxing champion George Foreman:

"For about 54 years, people have ask [*sic*] me not to keep saying "I love America" Well I do and I'm not ashamed. Don't leave it; Love it. Happy 4th of July." [7]

Keep the Light *of God's Grace* Burning!

---

[7] George Foreman (@GeorgeForeman) July 4, 2021

Personal Action Pages

Pray Through Isaiah 53:3-8 (NKJV)

[3] Do not let the son of the foreigner
Who has joined himself to the LORD
Speak, saying,
"The LORD has utterly separated me from His
people";
Nor let the eunuch say,
"Here I am, a dry tree."
[4] For thus says the LORD:
"To the eunuchs who keep My Sabbaths,
And choose what pleases Me,
And hold fast My covenant,
[5] Even to them I will give in My house
And within My walls a place and a name
Better than that of sons and daughters;
I will give them an everlasting name
That shall not be cut off.

[6] "Also the sons of the foreigner
Who join themselves to the LORD, to serve Him,
And to love the name of the LORD, to be His
servants—
Everyone who keeps from defiling the Sabbath,
And holds fast My covenant—
[7] Even them I will bring to My holy mountain,

And make them joyful in My house of prayer.
Their burnt offerings and their sacrifices
Will be accepted on My altar;
For My house shall be called a house of prayer for all nations."
[8] The Lord GOD, who gathers the outcasts of Israel, says,
"Yet I will gather to him
Others besides those who are gathered to him."

Ponder

1. How does God bless those who choose Him?
2. What does grace mean to you?
3. In what ways have you recognized God's grace in your life? In the life of others?
4. How has God shed His grace on America in the past? In the present?
5. What will it take for God to continue graciously blessing us?

Practice

- Find a way to express grace to someone you know.
- Find a way to express grace to someone you don't know.

Personal Observations

Chapter 9: Liberty In, Liberty Out[8]

Isaiah 61:1-2 (NKJV)

"The Spirit of the Lord GOD *is* upon Me,
Because the LORD has anointed Me
To preach good tidings to the poor;
He has sent Me to heal the brokenhearted,
To proclaim liberty to the captives,
And the opening of the prison to *those who are*
bound;
[2] To proclaim the acceptable year of the LORD,
And the day of vengeance of our God;
To comfort all who mourn,

Jesus quoted the above words from **Isaiah 61** in His sermon in the Nazareth synagogue found in **Luke 4**. The proclamation of liberty or freedom appeals to all who have been held captive. This appeal is true if we are the captives of sin or of sinful men. Why have so many people left California and other tyrannical states and headed for Florida? For freedom! Why are people coming to Christ with their addictions and distresses? For freedom!

---

[8] Clarkson, Kevin O. "1619 or 1620?" Liberty Church, 4 July 2021, Yukon, OK. Address.

God is the source of freedom for us. George Washington communicated to the Officers and Soldiers of the Pennsylvania Association, August 8, 1776:

> If we make freedom our choice, we must obtain it, by the Blessing of Heaven on our united and vigorous efforts . . . I trust that Providence will smile upon our Efforts, and establish us once more, the Inhabitants of a free and happy Country.[9]

While God is the source, we also play a role in our freedom. We are not passive in our quest for liberty but "vigorous in our efforts." Consider some of the ingredients of our freedom:

1. Freedom comes with the Spirit of the Lord. **2 Corinthians 3:17** (NKJV) reads:
   [17] Now the Lord is the Spirit; and where the Spirit of the Lord *is*, there *is* liberty.

2. Freedom comes with an inner awareness – **Luke 17:20-21** (NKJV)
   [20] Now when He was asked by the Pharisees when the kingdom of God would come, He answered them and said, "The kingdom of God does not come with observation; [21] nor will they say, 'See here!' or

---

[9] Federer, William J. *American Quotations*. Amerisearch, Inc., 2013, p. 557.

'See there!' For indeed, the kingdom of God is within you."

3. Freedom comes with an inner determination – **Galatians 5:1** (NKJV):
   Stand fast therefore in the liberty by which Christ has made us free, and do not be entangled again with a yoke of bondage.

4. Freedom comes with truth – **John 8:31-32** (NKJV)
   [31] Then Jesus said to those Jews who believed Him, "If you abide in My word, you are My disciples indeed. [32] And you shall know the truth, and the truth shall make you free."

Please notice that we are to abide, live in, and continue with the word of Jesus to know the truth so that truth can free us.

Thomas Jefferson has been attributed with the quote, "Eternal vigilance is the price of liberty." It is more likely that a man named John Curran coined it. Wendell Phillips elaborated on it in an anti-slavery speech in 1852:

Eternal vigilance is the price of liberty – power is ever stealing from the many to the few. The manna of popular liberty must be gathered each day or it is rotten. . . . [He went on to speak of the need for people to be aware of the potential for tyrannical rule and have a constant determination to stand against it.]

There is a vigilance involved in our freedoms. We must be

vigilant when dealing with sins that can rob us of our freedom. **James 4:7** (NKJV) is a reminder for us:

> [7] Therefore submit to God. Resist the devil and he will flee from you.

Notice that vigilance begins with a submission to God. Whether we are talking about a false gospel deceiving people, as Paul describes in Galatians, or an out and out attack on the souls of men, vigilance becomes an essential piece of our lives. It enables us to submit to God, to resist the devil, and to stand firm.

That same principle applies to our freedoms as Americans. Our Founders established America on the biblical principles that we can read in the Declaration of Independence and the U.S. Constitution. We obtained freedom by diligently submitting to God and resisting an evil empire in self-defense.

Similarly, we are engaged in that same kind of spiritual warfare today. We are fighting evil by submitting to God and then standing for Him. Freedom is not free or easy but well worth the price.

Keep The Light *of Liberty* Burning!

Keep The Light Burning!

Personal Action Pages

Pray Through Isaiah 61:1-3 (NKJV)

"The Spirit of the Lord GOD *is* upon Me,
Because the LORD has anointed Me
To preach good tidings to the poor;
He has sent Me to heal the brokenhearted,
To proclaim liberty to the captives,
And the opening of the prison to *those who are*
bound;
² To proclaim the acceptable year of the LORD,
And the day of vengeance of our God;
To comfort all who mourn,
³ To console those who mourn in Zion,
To give them beauty for ashes,
The oil of joy for mourning,
The garment of praise for the spirit of heaviness;
That they may be called trees of righteousness,
The planting of the LORD, that He may be glorified."

Ponder

1. What has held you captive? How did you gain freedom from it?
2. In what ways is God the source of our freedoms? Is there any true freedom apart from Him?

3. What is our role in gaining freedom?
4. How does "vigilance" fit in to our freedoms?
5. How does submission to God bring freedom?

Practice

- Ask the Holy Spirit to search your life and reveal anything that is being held captive.
- Make a game plan to gain freedom in Christ from this captor.

Personal Observations

Chapter 10: Freedom Lost— Freedom Found

Freedom is an inalienable right from God. God gave us freedom when He created humanity in the beginning. God made us in His image. As a result, we were to be the dominant species on earth. Nothing on earth was to be more significant.

God is the superior One with ultimate freedom. He can come and go as He decides. He can do what He wills. That was the image He had given us within the confines of the earth.

I wonder what it was like for our parents to have walked the earth in fear of nothing. I am sure you have personal fears like spiders and snakes, but they didn't. They were free of fear. They were free to be at the top of God's creation.

Something went wrong. We lost our freedom over a test of faith. God gave man one restriction, not to eat of one tree. We read in **Genesis 2:16-17** (NKJV):

[16] And the Lord God commanded the man, saying, "Of every tree of the garden you may freely eat; [17] but of the tree of the knowledge of good and evil you shall not eat, for in the day that you eat of it you shall surely die."

No doubt you remember the fall of man in **Genesis 3:1-7** (NKJV) [emphasis added]:

> Now the serpent was more cunning than any beast of the field which the Lord God had made. And he said to the woman, "Has God indeed said, 'You shall not eat of every tree of the garden'?"
>
> 2 And the woman said to the serpent, "We may eat the fruit of the trees of the garden; 3 but of the fruit of the tree which **IS** in the midst of the garden, God has said, 'You shall not eat it, nor shall you touch it, lest you die.'"
>
> 4 Then the serpent said to the woman, "You will not surely die. 5 For God knows that in the day you eat of it your eyes will be opened, and you will be like God, knowing good and evil."
>
> 6 So when the woman saw that the tree WAS good for food, that it **WAS** pleasant to the eyes, and a tree desirable to make ONE wise, she took of its fruit and ate. She also gave to her husband with her, and he ate. 7 Then the eyes of both of them were opened, and they knew that they WERE naked; and they sewed fig leaves together and made themselves coverings.

They had it all but gave into Satan, who spoke lies about God. The man now fell under the domination of sin. We read that Adam and Eve tried to hide from God in the Garden. Of course, they were unable, and soon God sent them out of Eden. God could not permit sinful people to eat of the tree of life and live forever as sinners!

Paul affirmed in **Romans 5:12** (NKJV) that the transgression of Adam brought sin into the world. He said:

Therefore, just as through one man sin entered the world, and death through sin, and thus death spread to all men, because all sinned. . .

With sin comes slavery. In the next chapter, he writes in **Romans 6:16-18** (NKJV):

[16] Do you not know that to whom you present yourselves slaves to obey, you are that one's slaves whom you obey, whether of sin LEADING to death, or of obedience LEADING to righteousness? [17] But God be thanked that THOUGH you were slaves of sin, yet you obeyed from the heart that form of doctrine to which you were delivered. [18] And having been set free from sin, you became slaves of righteousness.

Sugar is my foremost addiction. I am sure that addiction to alcohol or drugs must be horrific. But we can all be addicted to or servants of sin. That is, we become so engrossed in it that we practice it day and night.

God is greater. He can help us break that sin addiction or enslavement. THEN, we can be controlled by Him. In a sense, we become a "slave" or servant of God in that HE becomes the essential thing in our lives. It is not the sin that so easily besets us; it is Him.

You see, through Jesus, God frees us to a better life. He gives us liberty from the dominance of sin and its consequences. He said in **Romans 5:17** (NKJV):

> For if by the one man's offense death reigned through the one, much more those who receive abundance of grace and of the gift of righteousness will reign in life through the One, Jesus Christ.

We had freedom; we lost it and regained it in Christ. Guess what is still going on in the world? People are addicted to sin and so enslaved by it that they have no freedom. Only Jesus can end that loss of freedom and give us true freedom.

These are things our Founders understood. They knew that their first allegiance was to God. They knew that ultimate freedom was in Him. They also knew that they had to trust Him to break the chains of slavery forged by a tyrannical king. They trusted and experienced a foretaste of eternal freedom on earth.

Consider these quotes from our Founding era:
Benjamin Franklin**:**

> "Freedom is not a gift bestowed upon us by other men, but a right that belongs to us by the laws of God and nature."

Jedidiah Morse:

> "To the kindly influence of Christianity, we owe that degree of civil freedom, and political and social happiness which mankind now enjoy. In proportion, as

the genuine effects of Christianity are diminished in any nation, either through unbelief, or the corruption of its doctrines, or the neglect of its institutions; in the same proportion will the people of the nation recede from the blessings of genuine freedom and approximate the miseries of complete despotism."

Thomas Paine:
"Those who expect to reap the blessings of freedom must, like men, undergo the fatigue of supporting it."

Do you find it interesting that people under the control of Communism are fed up with that ideology, and many Americans want it here? Not only that, but in their illegal protests, they are waving American flags, a sign of liberty! Why is that? Because we founded our republic (not a democracy) on biblical principles, appealing to heaven in the process.

Where is your allegiance? Are you enslaved to sin or to righteousness? Peter speaks of false teachers in **2 Peter 2:19**, and points out that we are slaves to whatever controls us. He said:
¹⁹ They promise them freedom, but they themselves are not free. They are slaves of things that will be destroyed. <u>For people are slaves of anything that controls them</u> (NCV) [emphasis added].

Keep the Light *of Your Allegiance to God* Burning!

78

Personal Action Pages

Pray Through

Romans 6:16-18 (NKJV):

[16] Do you not know that to whom you present yourselves slaves to obey, you are that one's slaves whom you obey, whether of sin LEADING to death, or of obedience LEADING to righteousness? [17] But God be thanked that THOUGH you were slaves of sin, yet you obeyed from the heart that form of doctrine to which you were delivered. [18] And having been set free from sin, you became slaves of righteousness.

Ponder

1. What things do you fear? How will a close relationship with God alleviate fear?
2. Satan deceived our parents in the Garden. Where has he deceived you? What have you lost because of his deceptions?
3. How is our inalienable right to freedom tied to God?
4. In what ways is maintaining our freedom fatiguing?
5. How are we "slaves" to whatever controls us?

Practice

- Ask God to give you discernment so that you can know the truth from error.
- Begin improving your allegiance to God in the little things of your life.

Personal Observations

Chapter 11: Pursuit of Happiness

Philippians 4:4 (NKJV)

Rejoice in the Lord always; again I will say, rejoice.

There is a right way and a wrong way to seek happiness. Rejoicing in the Lord is always the right way. Jesus outlines our pursuit of happiness in the section we call the "Beatitudes" in **Matthew 5**. Yet, the concept is all through the Bible. In fact, in the case of the Beatitudes, the word "blessed" means "happy."

I like Benjamin Franklin's concept of the pursuit of happiness:

"The U. S. Constitution doesn't guarantee happiness, only the pursuit of it. You have to catch up with it yourself."

The Framers built the biblical concept of private property into our Constitution. As God began giving His Torah to Israel at Sinai, He speaks of private property in the Ten Commandments. Notice **Exodus 20:17** (NKJV):

[17] "You shall not covet your neighbor's house; you

shall not covet your neighbor's wife, nor his male servant, nor his female servant, nor his ox, nor his donkey, nor anything that *is* your neighbor's."

Ultimately, God owns everything. He does, however, allow us to be stewards of what is His in the form of what we call "private property." There is something special about our delegated ownership of property that encourages us to have the happiness we would not otherwise have.

Did you know that at one time in our history, the Pilgrims tried socialism? It failed, just like in all of the modern attempts at socialism! The Pilgrims set it up so that everyone was supposed to work. The farmers placed their crops in a community barn, and then as they needed food, they went and took what they needed. How do the Communists say it, "From each according to his ability; to each according to his need"?

It sounds appealing, but it doesn't work. You can guess what happened with the Pilgrims. They had shirkers even among their godly group. Some pretended to be ill and wouldn't work. Yet, they wanted to eat, and the workers resented working for the shirkers. Governor William Bradford said:

"Community of property was found to breed much confusion and discontent."

So, what was the solution? Private property and free enterprise! After all, the Bible says in **2 Thessalonians 3:10** (ESV):

". . . If anyone is not willing to work, let him not eat."

They divided the property into family plots, and each worked their plot as they wanted. They could use their products for food or barter. As a result, they went from near starvation to exporting corn.

Is it any wonder that people are streaming into the United States for freedom and property? Americans have had the chance to set their destinies by applying themselves to God's principles of economics as well as politics.

It is essential to know our history. It is essential to see that Socialism in any of its forms does not work, especially for our happiness. Isn't it interesting that none of the people clamoring for socialism in America are going to Venezuela or Cuba? Instead, they are trying to change

America. They think that we will be an exception to the rule in America. I wonder how people would feel if they lived in a socialist country for a year or two to experience it. Would they still want socialism with all of its shortages? Or, would they prefer free enterprise with unlimited possibilities? Which is biblical?

I'll close today with this quote I found on Facebook from a "Horrible World History" post.

> "Studying history will sometimes disturb you.
> Studying history will sometimes upset you.
> Studying history will sometimes make you furious.
> If studying history always makes you feel proud and happy, you probably aren't studying history."

Aren't you glad God works with us in our flaws to make us better? That's true as individuals. That's true as a nation. When we realize our accountability to God, we want Him to make us better people and clean up our flaws. The Pilgrims made a course correction and provided a clear example to follow.

Keep The Light *of the Pursuit of Happiness* Burning!

Personal Action Pages

Pray Through

The Beatitudes in **Matthew 5:3-10**

> [3] "Blessed *are* the poor in spirit,
> For theirs is the kingdom of heaven.
> [4] Blessed *are* those who mourn,
> For they shall be comforted.
> [5] Blessed *are* the meek,
> For they shall inherit the earth.
> [6] Blessed *are* those who hunger and thirst for
> righteousness,
> For they shall be filled.
> [7] Blessed *are* the merciful,
> For they shall obtain mercy.
> [8] Blessed *are* the pure in heart,
> For they shall see God.
> [9] Blessed *are* the peacemakers,
> For they shall be called sons of God.
> [10] Blessed *are* those who are persecuted for
> righteousness' sake,
> For theirs is the kingdom of heaven.

Ponder

1. How do the beatitudes relate to being salt and light in Matthew 5:13-16?
2. How do the promises Jesus gives compare to what the world pursues?
3. How do the beatitudes bring happiness to us?
4. Why does socialism fail?
5. How does private property help us pursue happiness?

Practice

Be more aware of the things God has entrusted you. What are ways you can be a good steward of those things?

Find 100 things for which you can give thanks to God today. How does this affect your happiness?

Personal Observations

Chapter 12: Absent Minded

Harold Urey was a Nobel Prize winner in Chemistry. One day, as he was walking along the street, he ran into another professor. They chatted for a few minutes, then, as they parted, Dr. Urey asked the other professor, "John, which way was I going when I met you?" "That way," said the other, pointing. "Oh, good. That means I've already had my lunch," muttered Dr. Urey as he walked away.

I am starting to get somewhat absent-minded myself. It seems like I "chase a lot of squirrels!" That's one of the advantages of growing older. We have a more acceptable excuse for forgetting things. I forget where I've left my keys, I forget others' names, and I sometimes forget why I have walked into a particular room. I call it the "Great Hereafter" – what am I here after?

On the one hand, there is an acceptable form of forgetting, much like Paul described in **Philippians 3:13-14** (NKJV):

> [3] Brethren, I do not count myself to have apprehended; but one thing *I do,* forgetting those things which are behind and reaching forward to those things which are ahead, [14] I press toward the goal for the prize of the upward call of God in Christ Jesus.

Paul had success and regret in his past, and he put those things behind him. He didn't wallow in those regrets or savor his past achievement. He forgot and looked ahead.

 On the other hand, there is an unacceptable form of forgetting—that is, forgetting God and His words. **Deuteronomy 8:11-14** (NKJV):

> [11] "Beware that you do not forget the LORD your God by not keeping His commandments, His judgments, and His statutes which I command you today, [12] lest—*when* you have eaten and are full, and have built beautiful houses and dwell *in them;* [13] and *when* your herds and your flocks multiply, and your silver and your gold are multiplied, and all that you have is multiplied; [14] when your heart is lifted up, and you forget the LORD your God who brought you out of the land of Egypt, from the house of bondage…

Moses was retelling the stores of God to the generation that was about to enter the Land of Promise. The older generation had died off and the younger was about to enter. Many of them had not seen what their parents and grandparents had, so Moses instructed them. Here, he especially instructs them not to forget God, that is, not to neglect His words and will.

This kind of forgetting is unacceptable because God doesn't forget us. **Isaiah 49:15** (NKJV) reads:

"Can a woman forget her nursing child,
And not have compassion on the son of her womb?

Surely they may forget,
Yet I will not forget you.

He does not ask of us what He will not do Himself. He says, "Don't forget me because I won't forget you." This kind of forgetting is also unacceptable because of undesirable consequences. **Deuteronomy 8:19-20 (NKJV) reads:**

[19] Then it shall be, if you by any means forget the LORD your God, and follow other gods, and serve them and worship them, I testify against you this day that you shall surely perish. [20] As the nations which the LORD destroys before you, so you shall perish, because you would not be obedient to the voice of the LORD your God.

In the founding of our nation, we almost forgot God. Benjamin Franklin refocused the delegates to the Constitutional Convention back to the One who brought us through the War for Independence. Remember his words?[10]

"I have lived, Sir, a long time, and the longer I live, the more convincing proofs I see of this truth--that God Governs the affairs of men. And if a sparrow cannot fall to the ground without His notice, is it probable that an empire can rise without His aid? . . . I therefore beg leave to move--that henceforth prayers imploring the assistance of Heaven, and its blessing on our deliberations, be held in this Assembly every morning

---

[10] Federer, William J. *American Quotations*. Amerisearch, Inc., 2013, p. 1124.

before we proceed to business, and that one or more of the clergy of this city be requested to officiate in that service."

When we didn't forget God, we were blessed. When we do forget Him, we struggle. This is a biblical principle and affects us just like Israel.

Someone has said, "I'd forget my head if I didn't screw it on tight." Christian, would you forget your head? Just don't forget who your head is!

During the Revolution, one of the slogans was, "We have no king but King Jesus!" So, as the writer of Hebrews admonishes, "Therefore we also, since we are surrounded by so great a cloud of witnesses, let us lay aside every weight, and the sin which so easily ensnares *us,* and let us run with endurance the race that is set before us, [2] looking unto Jesus, the author and finisher of *our* faith, who for the joy that was set before Him endured the cross, despising the shame, and has sat down at the right hand of the throne of God." (**Hebrews 12:1-2**, ESV).

Keep The Light *of Memory* Burning!

Personal Action Pages
Pray Through Deuteronomy 8:11-14 (NKJV)

[11] "Beware that you do not forget the LORD your God by not keeping His commandments, His judgments, and His statutes which I command you today, [12] lest— *when* you have eaten and are full, and have built beautiful houses and dwell *in them;* [13] and *when* your herds and your flocks multiply, and your silver and your gold are multiplied, and all that you have is multiplied; [14] when your heart is lifted up, and you forget the LORD your God who brought you out of the land of Egypt, from the house of bondage;

Deuteronomy 8:19-20 (NKJV)

[19] Then it shall be, if you by any means forget the LORD your God, and follow other gods, and serve them and worship them, I testify against you this day that you shall surely perish. [20] As the nations which the LORD destroys before you, so you shall perish, because you would not be obedient to the voice of the LORD your God.

Ponder

1. What is the power of memory?
2. How do you know God hasn't forgotten you?
3. What are the things you need to forget?
4. When are the times you need to remember?
5. How can you keep your focus on Jesus?

Practice

- Make a list of issues that have troubled you.
    - o Find a way to deal with them.
      Maybe restore a broken relationship by visiting with someone to "mend fences."
    - o Find a way to forget them.
      You might burn your list, bury your list, nail it to a cross, or some other similar exercise.

Personal Observations

94

Chapter 13: Sobriety Test

I am sure you know that if a police officer suspects you of drunk driving, they will pull you over and give you a sobriety test. They may even administer a blood test to determine the alcohol level.

The best way to avoid the consequences of drunkenness is to stay sober. If we are sober, we remain in our right minds, and our perceptions are not distorted. We can function appropriately.

The apostle Peter warns us about our adversary, the devil. He tells us in **1 Peter 5:8-9** (NKJV):

> [8] Be sober, be vigilant; because your adversary the devil walks about like a roaring lion, seeking whom he may devour. [9] Resist him, steadfast in the faith, knowing that the same sufferings are experienced by your brotherhood in the world.

Did you know that when lions stalk their prey, they do not want to roar – until AFTER they have killed it? A roar before would scare the prey away. However, they do roar afterward to frighten the packs of jackals or hyenas that may come around to take the prey from the lion. In fact, I have heard that the lion is actually afraid of packs of those animals because as a group, they can take down a lion with their sharp teeth.

Think for a moment about our evil adversary, "Satan" or the "devil." He doesn't send warnings about his presence. He hides it and stalks us covertly. Once he traps us, he can devour those who are unsuspecting. Right now, many people have fallen victim to him.

- A Satanic cult in Texas has demanded their religious right to practice abortion to use the aborted babies as sacrifices to Satan. They are being devoured.

- The BLM leaders not only admit to being godless Marxists, but they have also acknowledged participating in séances in which they call on the dead to inhabit their bodies. They are being devoured by a lie. Listen to God's truth in **Deuteronomy 18:10-14 (NKJV):**

> [10] There shall not be found among you *anyone* who makes his son or his daughter pass through the fire, *or one* who practices witchcraft, *or* a soothsayer, or one who interprets omens, or a sorcerer, [11] or one who conjures spells, or a

medium, or a spiritist, or one who calls up the dead. [12] For all who do these things *are* an abomination to the LORD, and because of these abominations the LORD your God drives them out from before you. [13] You shall be blameless before the LORD your God. [14] For these nations which you will dispossess listened to soothsayers and diviners; but as for you, the LORD your God has not appointed such for you.

- I understand that school children in California are being taught to chant incantations to four Mayan gods of human sacrifice. We can't pray to God in public school, but we can pray to demons. They are being devoured.

These are just three examples of the dominion of Satan in this world. He devours those who are overtaken by him. Did you notice that Peter tells us that not only is he the lion trying to devour but that we should resist him? What happens with resistance? He roars! He wants to frighten those who travel in packs to keep them under control.

Think for a moment about the recent "plan-demic." Don't think for a moment that the lockdown was about keeping you healthy. In my humble opinion, it was a means of controlling us by determining who could get out and who had to stay at home. Some government officials decided that bars were essential businesses, but gyms and churches were not. Gyms deal with the health of the body and churches with the souls. And what are bars good for? Police sobriety tests!

So, churches were shut down for weeks by government officials. But then some churches said, "No! We are going to meet." They defied the government and went back to worship. That's when the roaring started. Mayors and governors threatened them with fines and imprisonment.

In some cases, nothing happened. In others, ministers actually were jailed and fined. The dust has settled, and the lawsuits have been filed. The courts favor the churches and their ministers, not the government. The roaring ceases because the packs or communities of believers are standing up against the lion.

Satan is actually afraid of us. Like any bully, he bluffs and threatens. He has tried to make us afraid. But God has given us a Spirit of power, not fear, according to **2 Timothy 1:7**. That Spirit within us, which binds believers together, is more potent than anything Satan can throw at us.

Peter tells us to resist him. Look at what happens when we do in **James 4:7** (NKJV):

Therefore submit to God. Resist the devil and he will flee from you.

When believers unite against our mutual foe, we find strength and encouragement against him. Let's stand together for Jesus. Let's stand together for liberty.

Keep the Light *of Sobriety and Vigilance* Burning!

Personal Action Pages

Pray Through Deuteronomy 18:10-14 (NKJV):

[10] There shall not be found among you *anyone* who makes his son or his daughter pass through the fire, *or one* who practices witchcraft, *or* a soothsayer, or one who interprets omens, or a sorcerer, [11] or one who conjures spells, or a medium, or a spiritist, or one who calls up the dead. [12] For all who do these things *are* an abomination to the LORD, and because of these abominations the LORD your God drives them out from before you. [13] You shall be blameless before the LORD your God. [14] For these nations which you will dispossess listened to soothsayers and diviners; but as for you, the LORD your God has not appointed such for you.

Ponder

1. What are modern equivalents to making our children "pass through the fire?"
2. What are the dangers of the occult? How is our culture involved?
3. Why do you think these things are abominations to God?
4. What happens to God's people when they avoid the evils of the occult and only hold to Him? How do we benefit our society?

Practice

- Make a list of television shows, commercials, movies, etc. which are favorable to the occult. What will you do with these?
- How can you support the physical and spiritual well-being of our children?

Personal Observations

Chapter 14: Do We Love to Tell the Whole Truth?

Today, we hear a lot about being "loving" and loving people with whom we disagree. What does that mean? Modern culture's view of "loving" seems to be letting people have their way regardless of right or wrong. When our daughter was young, she would often threaten us with "not being happy" if we didn't give in to her way. But you know that you can't always give children what they want – even if they "won't be happy." Children don't always know what's best. Neither do adults, for that matter. **Jeremiah 10:23** (NKJV) reads:

> O Lord, I know the way of man *is* not in himself; *It is* not in man who walks to direct his own steps.

We also hear that we are unloving if we do not give people their way by endorsing specific biblically immoral issues. "Christians of all people ought to love everybody." There is truth in that. After all, Jesus said this was an essential characteristic of His disciples in **John 13:35** (NKJV).

> By this all will know that you are My disciples, if you have love for one another.

Some will ask, "Why shouldn't people of the same gender

be approved and encouraged to marry if they love one another?"

The <u>truth</u> is, we do not have the right or luxury to accept or endorse what God condemns. There comes a time when we have to speak truthfully in love (**Ephesians 4:15**). We do not love others when we go along to get along with people. We do not love if we do not warn them of the dangers to their souls. It takes speaking truthfully despite the consequences of not "making them happy" to show genuine love to people.

Imagine that you went to your doctor and he ran some tests. A few days later, you had a follow-up visit with your doctor. He told you that your blood pressure was normal, your temperature was as expected, and your heart rate was also normal. Your doctor didn't tell you that you had stage four pancreatic cancer.

The doctor let the lab contact you with those results. You go from feeling good about your health to feeling devastated. When you confronted your doctor, he said he loved you and didn't want to upset you, so he did not tell you about your cancer. That was not loving.

The apostle Paul lists the works of the flesh in **Galatians 5**. He then states in **Galatians 5:21** (NKJV):

I tell you beforehand, just as I also told *you* in time past, that those who practice such things will not inherit the kingdom of God.

Was Paul being loving or not? Modern Christians might not accept him. You see, if he were here today, he would make harsh "tweets" that don't sound very loving. But that is far from true. Paul's warnings were out of love for the people he wrote and those of us who read his words today. He asks in **Galatians 4:16** (NKJV):

Have I therefore become your enemy because I tell you the truth?

Even Plato knew it as well:

"No one is more hated than he who speaks the truth."[11]

---

[11] GoodReads, www.goodreads.com/quotes/7584407-no-one-is-more-hated-than-he-who-speaks-the-truth.

Benjamin Franklin said:

> "Freedom of speech is the great bulwark of liberty; they prosper and die together: And it is the terror of traitors and oppressors, and a barrier against them. It produces excellent writers, and encourages men of fine genius."[12]

We need the God-given freedom of speech to lovingly tell the truths of God to people.

The wise man, Solomon, stated in **Proverbs 18:21** (NKJV):

> Death and life *are* in the power of the tongue,
> And those who love it will eat its fruit.

We can lovingly speak the truth in hopes that people will learn and live. Or, we can be fearful and silent to let them flounder and die. We can lovingly speak the words of God, or we can be harsh, critical, and condemning. What we say or don't say; what we do or don't do WILL impact the lives, even the eternal lives, of those around us.

Yes, the consequences may be problematic. It is something for which we must prepare. But the words of God must not be compromised – either in spirit or in truth.

Keep The Light *of Loving Truth* Burning!

---

[12] AZ Quotes, www.azquotes.com/quote/1147827.

Personal Action Pages

Pray Through John 13:31-35 (NKJV)

[31] So, when he had gone out, Jesus said, "Now the Son of Man is glorified, and God is glorified in Him. [32] If God is glorified in Him, God will also glorify Him in Himself, and glorify Him immediately. [33] Little children, I shall be with you a little while longer. You will seek Me; and as I said to the Jews, 'Where I am going, you cannot come,' so now I say to you. [34] A new commandment I give to you, that you love one another; as I have loved you, that you also love one another. [35] By this all will know that you are My disciples, if you have love for one another."

Ponder

1. What have you experienced that proves we cannot "direct our own steps?"
2. How is it unloving to let our children make bad decisions?
3. How is it unloving NOT to tell the truth of God's will to people?
4. In what ways is it loving to kindly tell the truths of God to others?
5. How does the freedom of speech tie into teaching others the truth?
6. How does loving one another show we are disciples of Jesus?

Practice

- Think of people who have offended you by their words. How can you love them anyway?
- Think of people you have offended by your words. What can you do to show you love them?

Personal Observations

Chapter 15: A Few Too Many

1 Samuel 14:6 (NKJV)
> Then Jonathan said to the young man who bore his armor, "Come, let us go over to the garrison of these uncircumcised; it may be that the LORD will work for us. For nothing restrains the LORD from saving by many or by few."

A prominent theme in scripture is the "few." God often works through the minority rather than the majority. One reason for that is He wants to clarify where victory originates. It is not the capabilities of men but rather the power of God. He wants us to understand that He is more interested in faithful followers than majoring in numbers. Consider a few more verses on the "few":

Deuteronomy 7:7 (NKJV):
> The LORD did not set His love on you nor choose you because you were more in number than any other people, for you were the least of all peoples;

Matthew 7:14 (NKJV)
> Because narrow *is* the gate and difficult *is* the way which leads to life, and there are few who find it.

Matthew 22:14 (NKJV)
> "For many are called, but few *are* chosen."

Zechariah 4:6 (NKJV)
> . . "This *is* the word of the LORD to Zerubbabel:
> 'Not by might nor by power, but by My Spirit,'
> Says the LORD of hosts.

Isn't it amazing how God works? He acts so differently than we do. We think we need money and numbers (i.e., nickels and noses) to accomplish tasks. God rewards the opposite, the faithful few. Remember how he defeated thousands with Gideon's three hundred? Remember how He rebuilt Jerusalem and Israel with a remnant from Babylon? Remember how the handful of disciples "turned the world upside down" (**Acts 17:6**)? It was by His might and Spirit, not by the abilities of men nor great numbers.

I have read that a minority won our American Revolution. I have heard that one-third of Americans favoured separation from Great Britain; one-third opposed it, and one-third was neutral. Purportedly, three percent of the American population took up arms against the crown. A minority won liberty for the majority.

Abraham Lincoln included in his eulogy on Henry Clay, July 6, 1852, in Springfield, Illinois:
> On the fourth day of July 1776, the people of a few feeble and oppressed colonies of Great Britain, inhabiting a portion of the Atlantic coast of North America, publicly declared their national independence, and made their appeal to the justice of their cause, and to the God of battles, for the maintenance of that declaration. That people were few in numbers, and without resources, save only their own wise heads and stout hearts.

Today many faithful patriots feel like they are in the minority against the onslaught of evil that has gripped America and the world. Marxism in all of its forms is a

Satanic evil. The elites have imposed it on people worldwide and it is now in America.

According to George Barna and others, less than ten percent of American churches have a biblical worldview. Those with a biblical worldview use the Bible in EVERY aspect of their lives. The Bible is not just for worship or for going to heaven.[13] We must have a biblical worldview to combat the evils of Marxism.

If indeed we are the minority, we have a God who can win this spiritual war through the faithfulness of the few. WE can be the modern remnant that ushers in a new Great Awakening and turns the tide.

I want to encourage you today to stay faithful. Put on the whole armour of God. Do all you can to stand, and then pray, pray, pray! Who knows what all God is doing? We know that He wins in the end, and He brings the faithful few along with Him!

Keep The Light *of the Few* Burning!

---

[13] Shepherd, Josh. "Survey Finds Only 9% of Self-Identified Christians Hold to Biblical Worldview." *The Roys Report*, edited by Julie Roys, 10 Sept. 2021, julieroys.com/george-barna-survey-biblical-worldview/.

Personal Action Pages

Pray Through Deuteronomy 7:6-8 (NKJV)

[6] "For you *are* a holy people to the LORD your God; the LORD your God has chosen you to be a people for Himself, a special treasure above all the peoples on the face of the earth. [7] The LORD did not set His love on you nor choose you because you were more in number than any other people, for you were the least of all peoples; [8] but because the LORD loves you, and because He would keep the oath which He swore to your fathers, the LORD has brought you out with a mighty hand, and redeemed you from the house of bondage, from the hand of Pharaoh king of Egypt.

Ponder

1. In what ways does God think and act differently than we do?
2. Why do you think God chooses to work through a remnant so often?
3. How were the early disciples able to "turn the world upside down?"
4. How is Marxism linked to Satan?

Practice

- Research Marxism's tenets and make a side-by-side comparison to Christianity.
- In thinking of a biblical worldview, make a list of what you DON'T want Jesus to be Lord over in your life.
- Determine how He can be Lord over all of your life.

Personal Observations

Chapter 16: An Appeal to Heaven (Flag)[14]

Psalm 136:26 (ESV)

Give thanks to the God of heaven, for his steadfast love endures forever.

I am a "flag guy." I enjoy honoring our history by collecting some key flags. Since I don't have a flagpole, I have hung several in my garage for my enjoyment. A neighbor pointed out the "An Appeal to Heaven" flag on my wall the other day. I knew it was a flag of the American Revolution with an obvious connection to God, but I did not know the story. So I did some research.

During the early days of the American Revolution, before America adopted the famous "Betsy Ross Flag" as our national flag, several attempts at flags were made. We needed a way to distinguish the American forces from the British. One of the early flags was called the "Pine Tree" flag or the "Appeal to Heaven" flag.

The flag typically had a white background with a pine or cypress tree. The motto read, *"An Appeal to Heaven."* This flag was especially popular in the northern colonies. It

---

[14] "An Appeal to Heaven Flag." *Wallbuilders*, 15 Sept. 2020, wallbuilders.com/an-appeal-to-heaven-flag/.

incorporated the idea of the "Liberty Tree," a prominent symbol for independence in those colonies.

The Liberty Tree was a famous elm tree which stood near the Boston Common. In 1765 it was a rallying point for the first defiance against Great Britain. In time, further acts of rebellion began at the tree. A loyalist felled it in 1775.[15]

Thomas Jefferson used the phrase, "tree of liberty" in a letter to William Smith, John Adams' son-in-law, in 1787:
> [After describing the Revolution Jefferson went on to say,] ". . . God forbid we should ever be 20 years without such a rebellion. . . . And what country can preserve its liberties if their rulers are not warned from time to time that their people preserve the spirit of resistance? . . . The tree of liberty must be refreshed from time to time with the blood of patriots and tyrants. It is its natural manure. . . ."[16]

Jefferson appreciated and recognized the purpose and cost of liberty! When he used the phrase, "Tree of Liberty," he brought back the imagery of our rebellion against the forces of the tyranny of the English crown.

The origin of the Pine Tree flag's motto goes back to John Locke's SECOND TREATISE OF GOVERNMENT in

---

[15] "Liberty Tree." *wikipedia.com*, en.wikipedia.org/wiki/Liberty_Tree.

[16] "The tree of liberty... (Quotation)." *The Jefferson Monticello*, www.monticello.org/site/research-and-collections/tree-liberty-quotation.

1690. He explained that when government gets tyrannical, its citizens have the right to appeal to heaven and then resist through rebellion. He used Jephthah's words to the oppressive king of Ammon in **Judges 11:27-28** (NKJV) as a biblical proof text.

> 27"'Therefore I have not sinned against you, but you wronged me by fighting against me. May the LORD, the Judge, render judgment this day between the children of Israel and the people of Ammon.'" 28 However, the king of the people of Ammon did not heed the words which Jephthah sent him.

According to Locke and our Founders, once all appeals on earth are exhausted, and the only remaining appeal is to heaven, one must take a stand. Connecticut Governor Jonathan Trumbull asserted that the colonists made several to Great Britain, but the King rejected all. The pro-America preachers then filled their sermons with appealing to heaven and having a just cause for separating from England. Soldiers and sailors went into battle under the "Appeal to Heaven" flag to symbolize that they believed in God's Providence for their cause.

As we examine our history, we realize that we have needed to make "An Appeal to Heaven" even beyond the "American War for Independence." Time after time, we have found ourselves in difficult circumstances, and the ultimate appeal is to our God. Our appeal to heaven is true nationally, but it is also true individually.

How many times have you found yourself in need of divine aid? Maybe it has been a time of job loss. Maybe it is an illness. Maybe it is the loss of a loved one. Maybe you have found yourself in the pit of discouragement. No matter the scenario, we have always had a loving heavenly Father on whom we can depend. **Psalm 145:18** (NKJV) reads:

The LORD *is* near to all who call upon Him,
To all who call upon Him in truth.

Keep The Light *of Our Appeal to Heaven* Burning!

Personal Action Pages

Pray Through Psalm 136 (below is a portion, use your Bible for the rest)

Oh, give thanks to the LORD, for *He is* good!
For His mercy *endures* forever.
² Oh, give thanks to the God of gods!
For His mercy *endures* forever.
³ Oh, give thanks to the Lord of lords!
For His mercy *endures* forever:

. . .

²⁶ Oh, give thanks to the God of heaven!
For His mercy *endures* forever.

Ponder

1. How have you experienced the Providence (or "Provide–nce") of God?
2. When are the times you are most likely to make an appeal to heaven? How is the Tree of Liberty a symbol of America's "appeal to heaven?"
3. Why do you think revolution (not necessarily violent revolution) is necessary to maintain liberty?
4. Why do political leaders lose touch with the people? Why do they become enamored with power?

Practice

- Make a list and pray for our governmental leaders that we may have peaceful lives.
- Pray for wisdom to understand how to vote and how to stand against tyranny.
- Make a list of the times you cried out to God and how He responded.
- Create a symbol of your own "appeal to heaven." Use it as a reminder to pray.

Personal Observations

Chapter 17: Stand

Ephesians 6:13 (NKJV)
[13] Therefore take up the whole armor of God, that you may be able to withstand in the evil day, and having done all, to stand.

1 Corinthians 16:13 (NKJV)
[13] Watch, stand fast in the faith, be brave, be strong.

There comes a time in every person's life that shows whose side we are on. It is one of those watershed moments when we can no longer ride the fence. We have to declare where we stand. Years ago, I read this story about a famous baseball player named Brett Butler.

Brett Butler was a well-known baseball player. For years played for the Giants as one of their most popular players, and then his contract was up. He signed a free-agent contract with the L.A. Dodgers. They are the most hated rivals of the Giants. The first time the Dodgers came to San Francisco, the crowd didn't know what to do. Here was one of their more popular players wearing another team's colors. As he walked out on the field, some clapped, and some hissed. And then Brett Butler walked across the field and grabbed Tommy Lasorda, the manager for the Dodgers, and gave him a great big hug. And the crowd got angry and started booing. And he said, "Brett, why did you do that?" He said, "Because they need to know I've changed teams, and I'm a Dodger now."

We can go into the voter's booth and privately mark our choices for office. Would we vote any differently if we had to mark our ballots publicly? Most of us prefer to keep our important positions to ourselves. But, at some point, the secret is revealed. A person's beliefs come into full view. So will we stand with God?

When the children of Israel left Egypt, Pharaoh changed his mind about letting them depart. As his army approached them at the Red Sea, they feared being killed or captured. Moses declared in **Exodus 14:13 (NKJV):**

[13] And Moses said to the people, "Do not be afraid. Stand still, and see the salvation of the LORD, which He will accomplish for you today. For the Egyptians whom you see today, you shall see again no more forever."

While we may not understand all of the workings of God, we do understand that God works. What does He want from us? God wants us to stand with Him so that others will recognize us as His children. He wants us to stand out from the world of opposition to Him. Our whole civilization depends on it.

Years ago, President Ronald Reagan made this declaration:

"Our Pledge of Allegiance states that we are 'one nation under God,' and our currency bears the motto, 'In God We Trust.' The morality and values such faith implies are deeply embedded in our national character. Our country embraces those principles by design, and we abandon them at our peril. Yet in recent years . . . Americans . . . [have] for the sake of religious tolerance . . . forbidden religious practice in the classrooms. The law of this land has effectively removed prayer from our classrooms. How can we hope to retain our freedom through the generations if we fail to teach our young that our liberty springs from an abiding faith in our Creator?"[17]

God explained to the prophet why he allowed Judah to go into Babylonian captivity in **Ezekiel 22:30 (NKJV):**
> [30] So I sought for a man among them who would make a wall, and stand in the gap before Me on behalf of the land, that I should not destroy it; but I found no one.

No one stood for God. All blended into the background of the day. If there had been someone to stand, I wonder how things might have been different. I wonder what Judah would have looked like.

---

[17] "Remarks at a White House Ceremony in Observance of National Day of Prayer." *The American Presidency Project,* www.presidency.ucsb.edu/documents/remarks-white-house-ceremony-observance-national-day-prayer.

What would America look like if those professing to be followers of Jesus actually got serious and followed Him – out in the open? What would it look like if Christians lived out their faith and resisted evil by doing good? If Christians lived out their faith and stood up for the helpless? If Christians lived out their faith and voted according to scripture rather than their politics?

God wants us to stand with Him. He fights for us. He empowers us. We just need to stand and be recognized that we stand with Him. Jesus said in **Matthew 12:30 (NKJV):**

> [30] He who is not with Me is against Me, and he who does not gather with Me scatters abroad.

Again in **Matthew 10:32-33** (ESV):

> [32] "Therefore whoever confesses Me before men, him I will also confess before My Father who is in heaven. [33] But whoever denies Me before men, him I will also deny before My Father who is in heaven.

So, will we stand?

Keep The Light *of Standing for God* Burning!

Personal Action Pages

Pray Through Ezekiel 22:23-31

[23] And the word of the LORD came to me, saying, [24] "Son of man, say to her: 'You *are* a land that is not cleansed or rained on in the day of indignation.' [25] The conspiracy of her prophets in her midst is like a roaring lion tearing the prey; they have devoured people; they have taken treasure and precious things; they have made many widows in her midst. [26] Her priests have violated My law and profaned My holy things; they have not distinguished between the holy and unholy, nor have they made known *the difference* between the unclean and the clean; and they have hidden their eyes from My Sabbaths, so that I am profaned among them. [27] Her princes in her midst *are* like wolves tearing the prey, to shed blood, to destroy people, and to get dishonest gain. [28] Her prophets plastered them with untempered *mortar,* seeing false visions, and divining lies for them, saying, 'Thus says the Lord GOD,' when the LORD had not spoken. [29] The people of the land have used oppressions, committed robbery, and mistreated the poor and needy; and they wrongfully oppress the stranger. [30] So I sought for a man among them who would make a wall, and stand in the gap before Me on behalf of the land, that I should not destroy it; but I found no one. [31] Therefore I have poured out My indignation on them; I have consumed them with the fire of My wrath; and I have recompensed

their deeds on their own heads," says the Lord GOD.

Ponder

1. How does Ezekiel's passage remind you of the time in which we live?
2. What role does the person "standing in the gap" for the people play?
3. When do you feel uncomfortable in revealing your faith to people? Why is it important that you do?
4. What would America look like if those professing to be followers of Jesus actually got serious and followed Him – out in the open?
5. What would it look like if Christians lived out their faith and resisted evil by doing good?
6. If Christians lived out their faith and stood up for the helpless?
7. If Christians lived out their faith and voted according to scripture rather than their politics?

Practice

- Join a like-minded group of believers who want to unashamedly live for God.
- Find ways to kindly speak up for God when you have the opportunity.
- Learn to ask questions rather than give opinions.

- Include your children in doing acts of kindness for others.

Personal Observations

Chapter 18: A Bird's Eye View

Matthew 6:25-26 (NKJV)

[25] "Therefore I say to you, do not worry about your life, what you will eat or what you will drink; nor about your body, what you will put on. Is not life more than food and the body more than clothing? [26] Look at the birds of the air, for they neither sow nor reap nor gather into barns; yet your heavenly Father feeds them. Are you not of more value than they?"

One of the significant challenges for Americans is getting over being consumed by money and things. When Bill Clinton ran for president, he made a sign to remind himself, "*It's the economy, stupid.*" Isn't it interesting that the primary concern of Americans is having a robust economy year after year? Some even consider that forms of socialism and its ungodly ramifications will provide a form of economic security.

Yet, as mentioned in the opening passage, God repeatedly promises to take care of the people who follow Him. He took care of the millions of Hebrews for forty years in the wilderness, and they never missed a meal! What Americans (and all people) need is not just a healthy economy. We need God in America. When we seek Him, He responds.

Jesus uses the birds of the air to illustrate this point. The birds he describes were most likely on a migratory path between Africa and Europe. Israel was a rest stop where the birds could refresh and refuel on their journey. In the winter, they headed south. In the summer, they headed north. God provided even for the birds.

At the Constitutional Congress in 1787, Benjamin Franklin made a plea to the delegates who were having a hard time agreeing on a constitution for America. He appealed to them to pray and worship together as they had done during the conflict with England. He began his speech to the delegates with the birds:

> "I have lived, Sir, a long time, and the longer I live, the more convincing proofs I see of this truth--that God Governs the affairs of men. And if a sparrow cannot fall to the ground without His notice, is it probable that an empire can rise without His aid? . . ."

Congress decided to follow Mr. Franklin's advice and headed to church to worship and pray together. It was like someone flipped a switch, and the delegates almost miraculously came to a consensus on the Constitution. Delegates did not equate the Constitution to the same inspiration as scripture, but they felt divine providence with it.

It is funny how much we can accomplish when we aren't concerned about getting credit. It's even funnier what we can accomplish when GOD is first and foremost in the center of it. God is truly aware of the birds in flight and those that fall to the ground. He is undoubtedly aware of everything that is going on with our nation. We rise or fall within His sight.

When those early Americans trusted Him, He granted them independence from Great Britain. In so doing, they acknowledged their dependence on Him. On whom or what are we dependent?

I'm sure you feel it as well. The longer I live, the more I realize that every breath, every heartbeat, and every thought depends on God, who gives life and sustains life for His purposes. We think we are in charge. The truth is, God is. He is Creator and Sustainer. Just like the birds of the air, we need His provisions that come when we seek Him. Let's conclude with this reminder from **Acts 17:24-28** (NKJV):

24 God, who made the world and everything in it, since He is Lord of heaven and earth, does not dwell in temples made with hands. 25 Nor is He worshiped with men's hands, as though He needed anything, since He gives to all life, breath, and all things. 26 And He has made from one blood every nation of men to dwell on all the face of the earth, and has determined their pre-appointed times and the boundaries of their dwellings, 27 so that they should seek the Lord, in the hope that they might grope for Him and find Him,

though He is not far from each one of us; [28] for in Him we live and move and have our being, as also some of your own poets have said, 'For we are also His offspring.'

Keep The Light *of God's View* Burning!

Personal Action Pages

Pray Through Acts 17:24-28 (NKJV):

[24] God, who made the world and everything in it, since He is Lord of heaven and earth, does not dwell in temples made with hands. [25] Nor is He worshiped with men's hands, as though He needed anything since He gives to all life, breath, and all things. [26] And He has made from one blood every nation of men to dwell on all the face of the earth, and has determined their preappointed times and the boundaries of their dwellings, [27] so that they should seek the Lord, in the hope that they might grope for Him and find Him, though He is not far from each one of us; [28] for in Him we live and move and have our being, as also some of your own poets have said, 'For we are also His offspring.'

Ponder

1. What is Jesus' point in **Matthew 6:25-26**? Why do you think Jesus uses the birds of the air to make His point?
2. What does Paul emphasize about God in **Acts 17:24-28**?
3. How involved is God with the nations?
4. How hard is it to lay aside our need for recognition and competition?
5. How does prayer impact our worries and struggles?

Practice

- Reflect on issues which have worried you in the past. How did God help you cope?
- Make a list of the things that worry you. How can you "cast your cares on Him" (**1 Peter 5:7**)?
- In what areas of your life do you crave recognition? What would happen if you let that need go?
- With whom are you competing in your day-to-day life? What happens if you stop competing?

Personal Observations

Chapter 19: Our Prayer Guardian

Philippians 4:4-7 (NKJV)
[4] Rejoice in the Lord always. Again I will say, rejoice! [5] Let your gentleness be known to all men. The Lord *is* at hand. [6] Be anxious for nothing, but in everything by prayer and supplication, with thanksgiving, let your requests be made known to God; [7] and the peace of God, which surpasses all understanding, will guard your hearts and minds through Christ Jesus.

In 1849, Asiatic cholera spread through America. Approximately 4,500 people died in St. Louis, 3,000 in New Orleans, and 5,000 in New York City during the outbreak. Survivors buried many of them in a mass grave on Randall's Island. President Zachary Taylor proclaimed a National Day of Fasting, calling Americans to "humble themselves before His throne, and, while acknowledging past transgressions, ask a continuance of the Divine mercy." He urged them "to acknowledge the Infinite Goodness which has watched over our existence as a nation, and so long crowned us with manifold blessings, and to implore the Almighty in His own good time to stay the destroying hand."

On Friday, August 3, 1849, Americans filed into churches to unite in humility and prayer. By the end of the month, the death toll "dropped suddenly," and the plague abated.

We are living in an anxiety-filled time. We feel the chaos of evil and the feeling of helplessness that accompanies it. I recently read:

> The Anxiety and Depression Assoc. of America stated in the Washington Post on May 26, 2020, that 1/3 of all US citizens suffered from anxiety or depression during the pandemic. One-fourth of all middle school and high school students in America suffer from some level of anxiety disorders. Anxiety may be responsible for a whole host of physical problems: eating disorders, headaches, Irritable Bowel Syndrome, sleep disorders, substance abuse, Fibromyalgia, chronic pain, etc.[18]

God offers to bring us peace and a cure for our anxieties. It is prayer. Over and over, God reminds us that we can have a close relationship with Him. When we do, we realize that He is sovereign. The Lord is the One who fought for Israel, and He establishes our hope through the cross. He fights for us!

How important is prayer? Jesus said in **Mark 7:11** (NKJV) that His house should be a "HOUSE OF PRAYER FOR THE NATIONS" (**cf. Isaiah 56:7; Jeremiah 7:11**). Prayer is the priority of God's people. His house was not a house of preaching or singing but a house of prayer.

---

[18] Arch, Christopher, Remedy for Our Anxiety, Sermon Central, https://www.sermoncentral.com/sermons/god-39-s-remedy-for-our-anxiety-christopher-arch-sermon-on-stress-257868

Our Founders knew the importance of prayer. Often, colonial governors or the Continental Congress called for days of prayer, fasting, and humiliation. These times of prayer brought about noticeable results from the hand of God.

We have mentioned how Benjamin Franklin interrupted the chaos of the Constitutional Convention in 1787 to request times of prayer for the delegates. In part of that famous speech he said:

> "I therefore beg leave to move--that henceforth prayers imploring the assistance of Heaven, and its blessing on our deliberations, be held in this Assembly every morning before we proceed to business, and that one or more of the clergy of this city be requested to officiate in that service."

The prayers of those delegates guarded their hearts and minds. The Constitution came about rather quickly after they prayed.

Prayer was once the sustenance of America. During our Civil War, Abraham Lincoln admitted:

> "I have been driven many times upon my knees by the overwhelming conviction that I had nowhere else to go. My own wisdom and that of all about me seemed insufficient for that day."

Notice the final words of our birth certificate, the *Declaration of Independence* [emphasis added]:

"We, therefore, the Representatives of the united States of America, in General Congress, Assembled, <u>appealing to the Supreme Judge of the world</u> for the rectitude of our intentions, do, in the Name, and by Authority of the good People of these Colonies, solemnly publish and declare, That these united Colonies are, and of Right ought to be Free and Independent States; that they are Absolved from all Allegiance to the British Crown, and that all political connection between them and the State of Great Britain, is and ought to be totally dissolved;… And for the support of this Declaration, <u>with a firm reliance on the protection of divine Providence</u>, we mutually pledge to each other our Lives, our Fortunes and our sacred Honor."

If America is to continue, God must be present. To have His presence, we must sincerely pray and express our dependence on Him. Then, He will guard our hearts and minds through Christ Jesus, just as He did almost three centuries ago.

Keep The Light *of Prayer* Burning!

Personal Action Pages

Pray Through Philippians 4:4-7 (NKJV)

[4] Rejoice in the Lord always. Again I will say, rejoice! [5] Let your gentleness be known to all men. The Lord *is* at hand. [6] Be anxious for nothing, but in everything by prayer and supplication, with thanksgiving, let your requests be made known to God; [7] and the peace of God, which surpasses all understanding, will guard your hearts and minds through Christ Jesus.

Ponder

1. Who is the peacemaker in your family? How does he or she make peace?
2. On a scale of 1-10, how important is praying to you?
3. How often do you pray?
4. What are the primary contents of your prayers?
5. What is the most significant answer to prayer that you have experienced?
6. How does answered prayer affect you?

Practice

- Make your house (and/or church) a "house of prayer for the nations" by putting up a world map and praying through the countries.

- Find out as much information as you can about the countries for which you are praying and use it as a basis for your prayers.
- Make a list of your answered prayers and thank God for each one. Share your list with others if possible.

Personal Observations

Chapter 20: Know the Constitution

I want to loosely tie this chapter to **Psalm 119:11 (NKJV):**

> Your word I have hidden in my heart,
> That I might not sin against You.

I grew up going to public school. We knew nothing of homeschooling in my youth. Unlike now, those public school days weren't all bad. We still respected the Bible and the Constitution and American History in general back then. We were patriotic. Today our public schools are propaganda factories for the Communists who have taken over America. The emphasis is on compliance, not the "Three R's."

I have never been good at memory work. I especially had a hard time reciting from memory to the class. I have preached sermons and taught classes for over forty-five years. Still, I wouldn't say I like reciting from memory. If you ever are present for one of my classes or sermons, you will observe that I use notes for my presentations. I like to say that I am a "noted speaker" because I use notes.

Public school was helpful for me in doing memory work. In third grade, I memorized **Psalm 23**, **Psalm 100**, and the Lord's Prayer, all in the King James Version, of course.

Yes, that was in PUBLIC SCHOOL. Just try that now. In fifth grade, I remember memorizing a lot of America's documents. We memorized and sang patriotic songs. Probably the best thing I learned was the Preamble to the Constitution. After all these years, I can still recite it (at least at home where no one else is watching). By the way, my favorite Andy Griffith episode is the one where Barney thinks he knows the Preamble and tries to recite it. It's on YouTube if you need a laugh.

The Preamble reminds me of how the Ten Commandments introduce the Law of Moses and how the Beatitudes introduce the Sermon on the Mount. It is an outline of things to come. The Preamble sets us up for the "meat" of the Constitution. It's not a lengthy statement, but it is powerful. Here it is (and yes, I am copying and pasting it):

We the People of the United States, in Order to form a more perfect Union, establish Justice, insure domestic Tranquility, provide for the common defence, promote the general Welfare, and secure the Blessings of Liberty to ourselves and our Posterity, do ordain and establish this Constitution for the United States of America.

Notice some quick points:
- It starts with WE THE PEOPLE. Ours is not a top-down government but goes from below to above.

- It was intended to form a MORE PERFECT UNION. The Framers made allowances for the Constitution to be amended. It was not the most perfect, it was merely more perfect than what we had.
- ESTABLISH JUSTICE – How do you feel about the injustices going on today?
- INSURE DOMESTIC TRANQUILITY – How do you feel about those states that refused to stop the riots during the summer of 2020? There was nothing peaceful about burning buildings and citizens had no tranquility.
- PROVIDE FOR THE COMMON DEFENSE – This is why we have a military; not for conquest but for defense.
- PROMOTE GENERAL WELFARE – it is to promote it, not provide it (see **Deuteronomy 24**).
- SECURE THE BLESSINGS OF LIBERTY – Liberty is not unbridled freedom; it is freedom with responsibility. By the way, that responsibility begins with our personal responsibility to God.
- TO OURSELVES AND OUR POSTERITY – It was not just for one generation, but for future ones as well.

The downside to memorizing the Preamble is that I stopped there for years. I never read the entire Constitution until I was an adult. Have you read it? Suppose you served in the military or in certain other positions where you swore to defend the Constitution against all enemies foreign AND domestic. Did you know what you swore to defend? The Nuremberg trials outlawed, "I WAS JUST FOLLOWING ORDERS." We need to know what is lawful and what is not. Then we need to act accordingly.

Like most Americans, you know bits and pieces of the Constitution because you heard someone talk about such things as the First or Second Amendment. Most likely, though, you have never read it in its entirety. It does not take long, so read it. As you read, you will notice that the Constitution inadvertently mentions God. God is overtly within the Declaration of Independence. Yet, His fingerprints are all over the Constitution, like the Bible book of Esther.

Typically, we don't read the Constitution because we think we can't understand it. After all, lawyers who specialize in the Constitution debate issues that we laypeople can hardly begin to grasp. That is how many people approach the Bible. Some think that book is too difficult to understand. Instead of getting resources to aid in understanding, they just set the Bible aside.

What would happen if all Americans knew the Constitution and the stats of their favorite ball teams? What would happen if all Americans took the oath to formally or informally defend the Constitution? Do you think the politicians would be as open and bold as to ignore the Constitution as they are today?

For more information on understanding the Constitution, I would encourage you to check out Rick Green's website: **https://rickgreen.com/constitution-tools/constitution-classes/**

You can also go to the Hillsdale College site for online American heritage classes. The address is www.hillsdale.edu.

Keep The Light *of our Bible-Based Constitution* Burning!

Personal Action Pages

Pray Through Psalm 119:9-16 (NKJV)

[9] How can a young man cleanse his way?
By taking heed according to Your word.
[10] With my whole heart I have sought You;
Oh, let me not wander from Your commandments!
[11] Your word I have hidden in my heart,
That I might not sin against You.
[12] Blessed *are* You, O LORD!
Teach me Your statutes.
[13] With my lips I have declared
All the judgments of Your mouth.
[14] I have rejoiced in the way of Your testimonies,
As *much as* in all riches.
[15] I will meditate on Your precepts,
And contemplate Your ways.
[16] I will delight myself in Your statutes;
I will not forget Your word.

Ponder

1. In what ways have you seen the power of God's word?
2. How does it help keep us from sin?
3. What is the connection between our Constitution (and other founding documents) and the Bible?

4. How has public school changed over the years? Why do you think it has changed?

Practice

- Memorize the Preamble to the Constitution and reflect on its truths.
- Enroll in a class on the Constitution if possible.
- Find the biblical bases for Constitutional declarations.

Personal Observations

Keep The Light Burning!

Chapter 21: America, Who Are We?

I am somewhat naïve and probably too idealistic. When I think of America, I think of more than a set of borders on a map. I think of the idea of America. America is a place on earth where we incorporate values and ideals into the lives of its people. That place is where God is honored, and people treat one another as they want to be treated. That place is where any person, regardless of race, gender, or status, can become the person they want to be and make their dreams come true.

We may have had that America in our past, or at least an attempt at it. But we are certainly not there today. We have departed from the standards that built our nation.

Probably my greatest disappointment in America is the kind of people leading the country. They are no longer God-fearing servants of the nation. For the most part, they instead appear to be power-hungry bureaucrats, who, like the drug addict, have an insatiable drive for more.

We tend to elect leaders who reflect our values. Many, if not most Americans, appear to no longer hold the values of life, liberty, and the pursuit of happiness, and neither do our leaders. We have two sets of laws in America: one set with harsh consequences for the average American, and another set with little to no consequences for the elites.

Americans tolerate this divergence because we have lost our way.

Why does Congress have a different (and better) retirement system than the average worker in America? Why do they have a different (and better) healthcare system? Why do they appear to feel superior to their constituents?

What is the problem with auditing an election? Why should we fear the results if we have fair and honest elections?

Somewhere in our history, we got too busy to defend our liberties. Somewhere, we got too busy to audit the education of our children to see what our schools were and were not teaching them. Somewhere, we got lazy and decided that politicians and teachers knew better than moms and dads how we are to run our country and what we need to know for an education.

Somewhere, we got lethargic in our relationship with God. We decided that eternal salvation was our ONLY concern and left off the biblical worldview. Such a worldview says that God is Lord over EVERY part of our lives, not just worship services. That includes the church (with our eternal salvation), our families (with proper gender identity and morals), AND how the government should run the nation. All of those principles are in the scriptures.

We have abdicated our responsibilities. We have decided to let others be in charge because it is easier to complain than to question the answers.

I don't know if it is too late to reclaim America. We have indeed drifted to the waterfall and may soon be over the edge. The Marxists are in control of virtually every corner of our culture. However, God has a way of pulling out the stops at the last minute, like at the Red Sea. He has a way of retrieving His people when the going is most brutal, and the sky is the darkest. But He does not do those things in a vacuum of empty hearts.

God has specific requirements for His people. When we faithfully connect with Him, He acts on our behalf. There are always stated or implied conditions to His blessings for individuals and nations. What are some of those requirements? Two passages to consider:

2 Chronicles 7:13-14 (ESV)
> [13] When I shut up the heavens so that there is no rain, or command the locust to devour the land, or send pestilence among my people, [14] if my people who are called by my name humble themselves, and pray and seek my face and turn from their wicked ways, then I will hear from heaven and will forgive their sin and heal their land.

Micah 6:6-8 (ESV)

6 "With what shall I come before the LORD,
    and bow myself before God on high?
Shall I come before him with burnt offerings,
    with calves a year old?
7 Will the LORD be pleased with thousands of rams,
    with ten thousands of rivers of oil?
Shall I give my firstborn for my transgression,
    the fruit of my body for the sin of my soul?"
8 He has told you, O man, what is good;
    and what does the LORD require of you
but to do justice, and to love kindness,
    and to walk humbly with your God?

Jesus calls us salt and light. Doing the things God ordains enables us to be what God calls us to be.

Keep the Light *of Our Identity* Burning!

Personal Action Pages

Pray Through Micah 6:6-8 (NKJV)

> 6 "With what shall I come before the LORD,
>   and bow myself before God on high?
> Shall I come before him with burnt offerings,
>   with calves a year old?
> 7 Will the LORD be pleased with thousands of rams,
>   with ten thousands of rivers of oil?
> Shall I give my firstborn for my transgression,
>   the fruit of my body for the sin of my soul?"
> 8 He has told you, O man, what is good;
>   and what does the LORD require of you
> but to do justice, and to love kindness,
>   and to walk humbly with your God?

Ponder

1. How is America more than a location on a map?
2. What is the *idea* of America?
3. How do our elected leaders reflect the character of the nation?
4. What would it take to replace ungodly leaders with godly ones?
5. How have you seen **Proverbs 29:2** (NKJV) proved true?

When the righteous are in authority, the people rejoice; But when a wicked *man* rules, the people groan.

Practice

- Pray for the presence of God to fill the lives of the people you know.
- Pray for the presence of God to fill the lives of our political leaders.
- Pray and seek opportunities to share the gospel with people around you.
- Pray for ways to influence your world – church, schools, work, family, friends, etc.

Personal Observations

Chapter 22: Immigrants, Citizenship, and Excitement

Like the Apostle Paul in **Acts 22:28**, I am a citizen of my country by birth. The Roman tribune to whom he spoke had bought his citizenship. Millions have come to America over the years to obtain citizenship in our land. Perhaps you have attended or watched our new citizens inducted into America with their oath of allegiance.[19] That oath includes:

1. Renunciation of allegiance to former countries;
2. The support and defense of the Constitution and laws of the United States of America against all enemies, foreign and domestic;
3. Bearing true faith and allegiance to the same;
4. Bearing arms on behalf of the United States when required by law;
5. Performing noncombatant service in the Armed Forces of the United States when required by the law;
6. Performing work of national importance under civilian direction when required by the law;
7. Taking this oath freely, without reservation, and without any purpose of evasion.

---

[19] USA Citizenship Oath - US Immigration Blog (us-immigration.com)

There is no shame or embarrassment when these new citizens take their oath of allegiance. There is pride and excitement. No one is disrespectfully kneeling at the National Anthem, and no one is covering their head in their shirt. It is a celebration! People have often left modern tyranny and oppression to become part of the greatest nation in the history of the world. Here is freedom and the opportunity to become all we can be under God.

When Irving Berlin was five years old, he and his parents emigrated from a poor Russian Jewish ghetto and settled in the Lower East Side of New York City. Irving loved America and the opportunities he had here. He became a prominent songwriter.

In 1918, Berlin wrote, "***GOD BLESS AMERICA***." He revised it in 1938 as the Nazis began threatening all of Europe. Kate Smith sang the revision on her radio broadcast on Armistice Day. It became an immediate success, an "unofficial anthem of the US."[20]

Irving Berlin and millions of immigrants have loved America. People all over the earth look to us because God did shed His grace on us. How about us, dear patriots? What is our love for God's gift of America? It is harder for us, born into citizenship, to appreciate America as the new Americans do. The enthusiasm and gratitude of new

---

[20] Dr. Richard G. Lee, Gen. Ed. American Patriot's Bible (Dallas, TX: Thomas Nelson, Inc., 2009), p. 211.

citizens help us appreciate what we have been given – by God and the sacrifice of patriots through the years.

The excitement of new American citizens reminds me of our relationship with Jesus. New disciples act differently than the old ones. Do you remember how you felt when you discovered the "treasure hidden in the field" and that "pearl of great price" which Jesus described in **Matthew 13**? Now that time has passed, have you cooled off in your enthusiasm? Have you become a cynical critic rather than an excited servant?

As American disciples of Jesus, we need to remember what we have when "God shed His grace" on us. We attained freedom in Him as we followed. We experienced freedom in our country, again by God's grace and the sacrifices of patriots. Maybe the words to the church in Ephesus in **Revelation 2:4-5** fit here on two levels:
> [4] But I have this against you, that you have abandoned the love you had at first. [5] Remember therefore from where you have fallen; repent, and do the works you did at first. If not, I will come to you and remove your lampstand from its place, unless you repent.

No, America is not the new Israel or the actual kingdom of God on earth. Yet, it has been a blessed nation for which we can be grateful.

Keep the Light *of God's Blessing on America* Burning!

Personal Action Pages

Pray Through Revelation 2:4-5

[4] But I have this against you, that you have abandoned the love you had at first. [5] Remember therefore from where you have fallen; repent, and do the works you did at first. If not, I will come to you and remove your lampstand from its place, unless you repent.

Ponder

1. How do Americans and American churches compare to the church in Ephesus in **Revelation 2**?
2. Look up the lyrics to Irving Berlin's song "God Bless America."
3. In what ways is this song a second national anthem?
4. How does it reflect the feelings of legal immigrants to America?
5. How does it compare to YOUR feelings for America?
6. Where does God's grace fit in with America and our blessings?

Practice

- List times when God acted in American history.
- Write prayers that reflect your gratitude for His grace and mercy to us as a nation.
- Write a description of how America can renew a blessed relationship with God.

Personal Observations

Chapter 23: What Are You After?

If you are serving the Lord with all of your heart, I want to encourage you to keep going! If you have not yet begun that journey, I want to encourage you to get to know the Lord – from His heart to yours. **1 Samuel 13:14** (NKJV) reads:

> ¹⁴ But now your kingdom shall not continue. The LORD has sought for Himself a man after His own heart, and the LORD has commanded him *to be* commander over His people because you have not kept what the LORD commanded you."

Acts 13:22 (NKJV, explanation added,)

> ²² And when He had removed him [i.e., King Saul], He raised up for them David as king, to whom also He gave testimony and said, 'I have found David the *son* of Jesse, a man after My *own* heart, who will do all My will.'

The human heart weighs less than a pound. It beats about 100,000 times a day. Without your heart, your body would quickly die. In the Bible, the heart is the seat of emotions. It is the mind. It is the very essence and moral character of a person. So, when God says to love Him with all of our hearts, He says to love Him with the total capacity of everything we are.

Vance Havner wrote this on the importance of the heart:

"You may belittle experience and speak of the dangers of emotion, but we are suffering today from a species of Christianity as dry as dust, as cold as ice, as pale as a corpse, and as dead as King Tut. We are suffering, not from a lack of correct heads but of consumed hearts."

In our verses today, we see that David tried to be like God. He wanted the character of God within himself. We know that David was imperfect. But David's heart was such that even in his wrongdoings, he wanted to make the course corrections so that he would not only please God but also be like Him in his character.

David's heart is one of the reasons that God chose him to be king of Israel. David had some great attributes. David was handsome (**1 Samuel 16:12**), a courageous warrior (**1 Samuel 17**), and a protective shepherd (**1 Samuel 17:34**). While the sons of Jesse paraded by, Samuel looked on the outside while God looked within. God told Samuel in **1 Samuel 16:7** (ESV):

". . . For the LORD sees not as man sees: man looks on the outward appearance, but the LORD looks on the heart."

God has always worked this way. Whether it was choosing the most beloved king of Israel or the young virgin through whom His Son would come, God chooses the humble heart, not the superficially appealing. Mary sang Hannah's words in **Luke 1:46-48** (NKJV):

And Mary said, "My soul magnifies the Lord,
⁴⁷   and my spirit rejoiced in God my Savior,
⁴⁸ for he has regarded the lowly estate of his maidservant.

For behold, henceforth all generations will call me blessed;"

Let's go back to David. David pursued God during his lifetime. He went after the heart of God, and God rewarded him for it. Many people think that to follow God is to give up any exciting, meaningful life. If you look at the life of David, you know that is not true. What an adventure he had by seeking and following God. There was danger, trial, and challenge, as well as accomplishments!

Think of some key points of his life. For instance, God promised that he would be the king of Israel – even while Saul was king. God finally gave him the throne. His son, Absalom, stole the throne from him. David lived in exile but eventually returned to reclaim his rightful rule.

There are some parallels to Jesus for us. For eternity, God promised Jesus an eternal throne through the prophets. As we see in Revelation, there is a literal, eternal throne.

There is also a throne in each of our hearts. In some ways, the adversary has stolen that throne from Him. During the era of the American Revolution, Americans cried, *"No King but King Jesus!"* They wanted Him as king of their lives and nation.

Too many Americans have relinquished their allegiance to King Jesus. The evil one has stolen the hearts of many. Instead of Jesus, the adversary reigns in their lives. In a sense, they have exiled Jesus from themselves just like Absalom had done to David. Instead of honoring Jesus, they honor evil. We see it more and more today.

However, one day Jesus will return. He will re-establish His dominion and His kingdom forever. Everyone will see Him and confess Him as Lord and King (**Philippians 2:10**). Can you imagine how that will be? Can you imagine the end of the adversary and his followers? That day is coming.

The question in the meantime is: What are we seeking? What kind of hearts do we want? We sometimes talk of giving someone, even God, our hearts. Maybe we should be asking for God to give us His.

Keep the Light *of His Heart* Burning!

Personal Action Pages
Pray Through 1 Samuel 16:7-13 (NKJV)

[7] But the LORD said to Samuel, "Do not look at his appearance or at his physical stature, because I have refused him. For *the LORD does* not *see* as man sees; for man looks at the outward appearance, but the LORD looks at the heart." [8] So Jesse called Abinadab, and made him pass before Samuel. And he said, "Neither has the LORD chosen this one." [9] Then Jesse made Shammah pass by. And he said, "Neither has the LORD chosen this one." [10] Thus Jesse made seven of his sons pass before Samuel. And Samuel said to Jesse, "The LORD has not chosen these." [11] And Samuel said to Jesse, "Are all the young men here?" Then he said, "There remains yet the youngest, and there he is, keeping the sheep." And Samuel said to Jesse, "Send and bring him. For we will not sit down till he comes here." [12] So he sent and brought him in. Now he *was* ruddy, with bright eyes, and good-looking. And the LORD said, "Arise, anoint him; for this *is* the one!" [13] Then Samuel took the horn of oil and anointed him in the midst of his brothers; and the Spirit of the LORD came upon David from that day forward. So Samuel arose and went to Ramah.

Ponder

1. What is the significance of our hearts to God?
2. How was David's heart different than most?
3. What characteristics of David do you identify with?
4. Why do you think God chooses the *HUMBLE* heart to be His servant?
5. How are humility and confidence linked?

Practice

- Ask the Holy Spirit to reveal your true heart.
- Make a list of your positive qualities. Find ways that you can enhance those qualities.
- Make a list of areas in which you need to improve.
- Use a topical Bible and read verses that apply to you. How can you put those verses into action?

Personal Observations

Chapter 24: Godless Communism

The Nazi Party of Germany was their National Socialist Party. The German people willingly gave up their inalienable rights for some perceived security from the Nazis. Power rested in the hands of an elite few, especially Adolf Hitler. Do you find it ironic that a Jewish American like Bernie Sanders wants to be a National Socialist after all the Jewish people suffered?

The controlling Nazi powers convinced the Germans to commit or at least to allow incredible atrocities. The German people oppressed and exterminated millions of innocent people, both Jews and non-Jews. By the time the German population began waking up to the realities of National Socialism, it was too late to change it. The evil was so entrenched that it would take the hand of God to remove it.

You may recall the Nuremberg Trials where officials of the Nazi Party were arrested and put on trial for killing millions of Jews and others in the Holocaust. The Nuremberg Trials of 1945-1946 displayed the socialistic idea that rights come from the "group" and not from God. Nazi officials defended their actions by explaining they were only following laws agreed upon by the people of the German state.

Nazi General Hans Frank provided insight into the perpetrators' mindset. Frank carried out orders to plunder Poland and commit the mass murder of millions of Poles and Jews in death camps. At his trial, August 31, 1945, Hans Frank was remorseful as he described the false justification for his acts and the slippery slope of socialist thought:

> At the beginning of our way we did not suspect that our turning away from God could have such disastrous deadly consequences and that we would necessarily become more and more deeply involved in guilt. At that time we could not have known that so much loyalty and willingness to sacrifice on the part of the German people could have been so badly directed by us. Thus, by turning away from God, we were overthrown and had to perish …

Frank continued:

> Before all, God pronounced and executed judgment on Hitler and the system which we served with minds far from God. . . We call upon the German people … to return from this road which, according to the law and justice of God, had to lead us and our system into disaster and which will lead everyone into disaster who tries to walk on it… everywhere in the whole world.[21]

---

[21] William J. Federer, Socialism: The Real History from Plato to the Present, pp. 100-101.

Did you notice that Frank said they had left God? And that God pronounced and executed judgment on Hitler and the Nazi system? Socialism and communism are atheistic forms of government that deviate from God's ways. THEY become a god dictating who lives and who dies; who has rights and who doesn't.

Socialism always leads to communism. Someone said that communism is socialism with a gun. Ever wonder why our anti-American politicians want to collect your firearms and destroy the Second Amendment? It's because they want the weapons and don't want you to have the inalienable right to defend yourself. Look again at Australia. Those poor folks are shut down in their houses and carried off to concentration camps or "Wellness Camps," as they say. They cannot defend themselves because the Socialists have taken their weapons. Our Founders and Framers understood the need to defend our homes from oppressive government and built that self-defense into the Constitution. They lived it with the tyrannical King George.

We desperately need God in America. In many ways we are following the same path of others who forgot Him. What was their result? According to Hans Frank, it was divine justice. Before his execution as a war criminal, a Roman Catholic priest taught him the gospel. He repented of his atrocities. We'll leave eternal judgment up to God, but even though he converted to a form of Christianity, he still had to pay for his actions.

In part **Deuteronomy 8:11-20** (ESV) reads:

[11] "Take care lest you forget the LORD your God by not keeping his commandments and his rules and his statutes, which I command you today, [12] lest, when you have eaten and are full and have built good houses and live in them, [13] and when your herds and flocks multiply and your silver and gold is multiplied and all that you have is multiplied, [14] then your heart be lifted up, and you forget the LORD your God, who brought you out of the land of Egypt, out of the house of slavery, . . . [17] Beware lest you say in your heart, 'My power and the might of my hand have gotten me this wealth.' . . . [19] And if you forget the LORD your God and go after other gods and serve them and worship them, I solemnly warn you today that you shall surely perish. [20] Like the nations that the LORD makes to perish before you. . ."

It happened to Israel. It happened to Germany. It happened to other nations who forgot God. Do you think it won't happen to America? So, what do we do? God answers in **Deuteronomy 11:18-21** (ESV):

[18] "You shall therefore lay up these words of mine in your heart and in your soul, and you shall bind them as a sign on your hand, and they shall be as frontlets between your eyes. [19] You shall teach them to your children, talking of them when you are sitting in your house, and when you are walking by the way, and when you lie down, and when you rise. [20] You shall write

them on the doorposts of your house and on your gates, [21] that your days and the days of your children may be multiplied in the land that the LORD swore to your fathers to give them, as long as the heavens are above the earth."

God and His words should saturate our lives. We should be able to say, as Jesus did in **Matthew 4 and Luke 4**, "It is written," to follow the will of God and avoid the many temptations we face.

We don't want our children and grandchildren living under disastrous systems of government like socialism or communism. These only bring pain and suffering for the citizens. We need to know God, and we need to pass that knowledge onto our descendants. He is the source of life (**John 10:10**); liberty (**Galatians 5:1**), and the pursuit of happiness (**Matthew 5:1-12**).

Keep The Light *of Freedom* Burning!

Personal Action Pages

Pray Through Deuteronomy 11:11-21 (ESV):

[11] "Take care lest you forget the LORD your God by not keeping his commandments and his rules and his statutes, which I command you today, [12] lest, when you have eaten and are full and have built good houses and live in them, [13] and when your herds and flocks multiply and your silver and gold is multiplied and all that you have is multiplied, [14] then your heart be lifted up, and you forget the LORD your God, who brought you out of the land of Egypt, out of the house of slavery, . . . [17] Beware lest you say in your heart, 'My power and the might of my hand have gotten me this wealth.' . . . [19] And if you forget the LORD your God and go after other gods and serve them and worship them, I solemnly warn you today that you shall surely perish. [20] Like the nations that the LORD makes to perish before you. . . .

[18] "You shall therefore lay up these words of mine in your heart and in your soul, and you shall bind them as a sign on your hand, and they shall be as frontlets between your eyes. [19] You shall teach them to your children, talking of them when you are sitting in your house, and when you are walking by the way, and when you lie down, and when you rise. [20] You shall write them on the doorposts of your house and on your gates, [21] that your days and the days of your children

may be multiplied in the land that the LORD swore to your fathers to give them, as long as the heavens are above the earth.

Ponder

1. What happens when we forget God?
2. How do we forget God?
3. How can we prevent ourselves from forgetting God?
4. How do you think the Nazis and the German people forgot God? Can that happen to America?

Practice

- Make a plan of things you can do to keep a close relationship with God.
- Teach your children biblical principles. It will help them and reinforce God's truths for you.
- As you teach your children, do so in a way they can understand. **Proverbs 22:6** (NKJV) reads:
  Train up a child in the way he should go,
  And when he is old he will not depart from it.
- Make a list of ways you can teach your children (or others) throughout the day.

Personal Observations

Chapter 25: Law and Order

Matthew 24:12-14 (NKJV)

[12] And because lawlessness will abound, the love of many will grow cold. [13] But he who endures to the end shall be saved. [14] And this gospel of the kingdom will be preached in all the world as a witness to all the nations, and then the end will come.

Jesus points out how essential the teachings of God are to society. When Israel was faithful to the teachings, they conquered and were prosperous. When they deviated from those words, their enemies conquered them.

We translate the word "Law" (as in the 'Law' of Moses) from the word "Torah." Torah includes the commands and rules of God, but it is more. We can better translate "Torah" as "teachings" or "instructions." That gives it a whole different connotation. Indeed, God gives commands that we are to obey. But He also gives teachings that have nothing to do with salvation, which will enhance our lives.

Consider that when Jesus speaks about "lawlessness," He isn't merely referring to violating the civil codes of a community or nation. He is talking about people who are "Torah-less." That is, they live without the teachings or instructions of God.

When we ignore the teachings of God or rebel against them as the current Marxist groups are doing, we open the door to decadence within our society. We ignore God and reject His words. If we create such a vacuum, what will fill it? Only wickedness of every kind! God will not hold us guiltless for unrepented wickedness but will reveal His wrath upon it as we see in **Romans 1**.

Right now in America, we are in a spiritual war. Many Christians are finally waking up to the realities of Good vs. Evil. They finally see the corruption on all levels of our nation. They are finally praying as never before! We are aware now, more than ever, of the distress in **Isaiah 5:20** (NKJV):

> Woe to those who call evil good, and good evil;
> Who put darkness for light, and light for darkness;
> Who put bitter for sweet, and sweet for bitter!

Jesus points out in **Matthew 24:12** that when we ignore God's words, our love grows cold. Have you noticed it? Love for God is on the decline. More and more attempts to undermine the scriptures are happening. Once, both political parties acknowledged God and wanted His direction. Today, one of those parties has officially excluded Him from their platform. The other gives lip service to Him and renounces Him by their behavior in the political back rooms.

Have you noticed the growing anger and hatred among Americans? Racial tensions are mounting. Marxists have introduced the Critical Race Theory to our schools. Their purpose is to divide in order to conquer. The division is on every hand so that there's not much *"Love thy neighbor as thyself"* anymore. By the way, that <u>is</u> the answer to overcoming all of this tension and anger. If we break the cycle of hate with love, we will push back the evil. It is challenging to love enemies and those who hate you, but it is biblical. It is what a disciple of Jesus does.

Love HAS grown cold because people do not want to acknowledge the presence of God. If we acknowledge His presence, He compels us to hear Him. If we reject or ignore Him, we feel safe in our cabal, our *"den of thieves"* (**Jeremiah 7:11**). But there is a day of reckoning coming. Hiding in our presumably safe places outside the will of God won't benefit us. God sees what we do. God knows the hearts of men. We will be held accountable.

Our national ancestors understood their place before God. They knew that He was aware of their actions. They tried to live knowing they were accountable to Him. So, when we pledge, *"One nation UNDER God,"* there is a reason. National independence from tyranny begins with personal dependence on God and accountability to Him.

That kind of conscience is absent today among many Americans. We have forgotten the word of God and failed in our knowledge of Him. Just observe all of the elements attached to the election fraud of November 2020. The evidence points at national and international conspiracies to cheat. They have attempted cover-ups. There are no indications of conscience among the guilty. To them, the ends justify the means.

Jesus reminds us in **Matthew 24:35** that heaven and earth will pass away, but His words will remain – forever. Nations rise and fall by His will. To succeed as a nation, we MUST build and maintain it on the word of God. Our Founders attempted this. Some have attributed the following quote to James Madison:

> "We have staked the whole future of American civilization, not upon the power of government, far from it. We have staked the future of all of our political institutions upon the capacity of each and all of us to govern ourselves, to control ourselves, to sustain ourselves according to the Ten Commandments of God."

Keep the Light *of God's Word* Burning!

Personal Action Pages

Pray Through Matthew 24:9-14 (NKJV)

[9] "Then they will deliver you up to tribulation and kill you, and you will be hated by all nations for My name's sake. [10] And then many will be offended, will betray one another, and will hate one another. [11] Then many false prophets will rise up and deceive many. [12] And because lawlessness will abound, the love of many will grow cold. [13] But he who endures to the end shall be saved. [14] And this gospel of the kingdom will be preached in all the world as a witness to all the nations, and then the end will come.

Ponder

1. What is the relationship between removing God's Law and love growing cold?
2. What are the personal effects of ignoring or rejecting the word of God?
3. What are the national effects of ignoring or rejecting the word of God?
4. How does one affect the other?
5. What happens if we do not repent of sin? Nationally? Personally?

Practice

- Create some reminders that you are accountable to God throughout your day.
    - Set an alarm to pray at certain times during the day.
    - Associate locations with godly actions you can do such as serving people in your workplace by doing random acts of kindness.

- Set times to strengthen your biblical knowledge as the Bereans in **Acts 17:11** (NKJV) did so that you are not deceived by false teachers.
    [11] These were more fair-minded than those in Thessalonica, in that they received the word with all readiness, and searched the Scriptures daily *to find out* whether these things were so.

- Make a visual display to remind yourself that we are *"one nation under God."*

Personal Observations

Chapter 26: Keeping the Republic

You may be like me and have grown a bit tired of hearing the story of Mrs. Powell, the wife of Philadelphia's mayor, and Benjamin Franklin after the Constitutional Convention. The story goes, that on September 19, 1787, after the Constitutional Convention endorsed the final form of the Constitution, Benjamin Franklin went outside the hall in Philadelphia and was asked by Mrs. Powell:

> "Well Doctor, what have we got, a republic or a monarchy?" Franklin replied: "A republic if you can keep it."[22]

In recent months I have heard that story repeated by many earnest speakers regarding the future of our nation. Some butcher the story, and some get it right. No matter how many times we hear, we need to hear the point.

A republic is hard to keep because the government is "of the people, by the people, and for the people," and people have issues. The people have a strong obligation in our republic to get involved in the politics of our government. People also have a responsibility to live up to the principles inherent in the republic. Otherwise, the republic will fall.

---

[22] Bartlett's Familiar Quotations, Sixteenth Edition, at 310:26, referenced under "A republic, if you can keep it."

We know that our Founders and Framers envisioned and established a unique republic. They saw our responsibility before God and established a republic based on Him and His word. France, for instance, established a godless republic after we established ours. Instead of basing it on God, they based it on man.

The French rebelled against God and faith in their new republic. Instead of using "the year of our Lord" on documents, for instance, they started a new calendar with the first year of their republic as "Year One." They replaced the Bible's seven-day week with a ten-day week and a ten-month year. They banned crosses as offensive, destroyed religious monuments, outlawed public and private worship, executed priests and ministers on sight, desecrated Christian graves, and closed churches. French protesters even used some of the sacred places for depraved purposes.[23]

So, what is so important about <u>our</u> republic? Why should we fight to keep it? Are we different than France and the Union of Soviet Socialist Republics?

Our republic was based on the Bible and followed the example of God's intentions for Israel. We know Israel did not always live up to God's expectations, and neither do

---

[23] William J. Federer, Socialism: The Real History from Plato to the Present, pp. 68-72.

we. Thank God He does not cast us off in our offenses but is "longsuffering/patient, not willing that any should perish" (**2 Peter 3:9**). Consider some examples of Israel that we imitated through the word of God.

1. **No King but God**. Yes, they had a leader, Moses, when they left Egypt but did not select a king for years. God intended to be their King.

2. **Equality**. With no king or royal family, everyone was equal before God. Christians have a saying, "The ground is level at the foot of the cross." That concept was genuine then and now. There are rules for the elites in modern America and rules for us commoners. We are not equal under the law right now. That was never God's intention or that of our Founders and Framers. God said in **Deuteronomy 1:17** (NKJV):

   > [7] You shall not show partiality in judgment; you shall hear the small as well as the great; you shall not be afraid in any man's presence, for the judgment *is* God's. The case that is too hard for you, bring to me, and I will hear it.'

3. **Private Property**. Of course, everything belongs to the LORD (**Psalm 24:1**). Still, when God sent the people into the Land, He gave them perpetual private property (see **Exodus 20:15, 17**). With that property came the potential to amass wealth. The Bible calls it "blessings." Karl Marx opposed private property. In his *Manifesto*, he summed up the theory of the Communists in the abolishment of private property. Our Republic endorsed private

property like Israel and unlike the godless Communists.

4. **Welfare System**. **Leviticus 19:9-10** describes the welfare system of Israel. America has always had a benevolent heart as part of our biblical DNA. God compelled Israel to care for the poor. He compels us, too, because we have followed the same teachings. Indeed, our welfare system could use an overhaul, but the spirit is there to care for those in need (see **James 1:27**).

5. **Choosing Leaders**. Honest elections allowed for government by the consent of the governed (we would say, "of, by, and for the people"). Read **Deuteronomy 1:3-13** (NKJV) and notice especially **verse 13**:

> [13] Choose wise, understanding, and knowledgeable men from among your tribes, and I will make them heads over you.'

Time doesn't permit a full rehearsal of all the similarities between Israel and America. These few help us grasp the importance of keeping a godly republic, not just a republic. The work of maintaining our republic involves knowing and obeying the scriptures. **John Adams** said that our Constitution was fit only for moral and religious people. That is true today, too.

That work involves vigilance in what is going on in our schools, our communities, and our governments. We can no longer allow our leaders the luxury of no accountability. Is it any wonder why the Marxists got rid of prayer and Bible study from our public schools? But why did we go along with it? Why didn't we fight to keep our republic?

There is no doubt that we are in a fight for the soul of America right now. I want to encourage you to pray, to equip yourselves with the whole armor of God, and to stand together against the onslaught of the dissemination of evil in our land. Our republic is worth fighting for, because it can be a foretaste of the eternal rule of Jesus and the betterment of all humanity through Him when done correctly.

Keep The Light *of Our Republic* Burning!

Personal Action Pages

Pray Through Deuteronomy 1:9-13 (NKJV)

[9] "And I spoke to you at that time, saying: 'I alone am not able to bear you. [10] The LORD your God has multiplied you, and here you *are* today, as the stars of heaven in multitude. [11] May the LORD God of your fathers make you a thousand times more numerous than you are, and bless you as He has promised you! [12] How can I alone bear your problems and your burdens and your complaints? [13] Choose wise, understanding, and knowledgeable men from among your tribes, and I will make them heads over you.'"

Ponder

1. How is God (or Jesus) our King?
2. What is the difference between a republic and a democracy? Why is a republic more valuable?
3. Why is it hard to "keep" a republic?
4. How does a republic under God reflect biblical principles?
5. How can we use God's weapons to defend our republic (**Ephesians 6:10-20**)?

Practice

- Practice holding your elected officials accountable for their votes and actions.
- Get involved with groups that are promoting American ideals such as the John Birch Society or other groups.
- Make a list of the "compartments" of your life like family, work, church, recreation, etc. Identify the area(s) in which Jesus is NOT Lord. Make a plan to have Jesus as Lord over all of your life.

Personal Observations

Call to Action

Several years ago, I heard the following humorous illustration:

The doctor shook his head. "John, you're in terrible shape. You've got to do something, and I mean starting today. First, I want you to tell your wife to cook more nutritious meals. I want you to stop working like a dog. Tell your wife you're going to make a budget, and she has to stick to it. And have her keep the kids off your back so you can relax. Unless there are some changes in your life, you'll be dead in a month."

"Doc," John said, "this would sound more official coming from you. Could you please call my wife and give her those instructions?' "OK."

When John got home, his wife rushed to him and began to weep on his shoulder. "Oh, honey, I talked to the doctor. You poor man – he says you have only thirty days to live!"

The crux of this book is to keep God's light burning in

every area of our lives. Is there an area of your life do you NOT want God to rule? Whatever area that area may be, is your idol. Your idol could be your children and their ball games. It could be your job, leisure time, or even politics. God's light needs to shine everywhere!

Ecclesiastes 12:13 (NKJV) reads:

¹³ Let us hear the conclusion of the whole matter:

Fear God and keep His commandments,
For this is man's all.

Life boils down to a matter of priorities. To "keep the light burning" means we make God's light our priority. We live with the intentionality of bringing His light into every situation of our lives.

Too often, Christians are ashamed for people to know they are followers of Jesus. They would prefer to shrink into the background rather than stand for Jesus. Jesus reminds us of this severe neglect in **Mark 8:38** (NKJV). He warns us:

For whoever is ashamed of Me and My words in this adulterous and sinful generation, of him the Son of Man also will be ashamed when He comes in the glory of His Father with the holy angels.

Solomon reminds us that the priority of life is God, not myself. God is not interested in how convenient my life might be. I might seek luxury or entertainment, but God doesn't. God has a higher calling for my life, my faithful obedience. My reverential obedience brings satisfaction that nothing else can.

God has given us everything. He did not stop with temporal blessings. God the Father gave us His Son and the opportunity to share eternity with Him. He wants us to make Him our life's top priority.

Romans 8:32 (NKJV) reminds us of God's gracious gifts. Paul wrote:

> *He who did not spare His own Son, but delivered Him up for us all, how shall He not with Him also freely give us all things?*

If we are the recipients of such gifts from God, how should we act? **John 14:21** (NKJV) reminds us of our responsibility.

> *He who has My commandments and keeps them, it is he who loves Me. And he who loves Me will be loved by My Father, and I will love him and manifest Myself to him.*

I think C. S. Lewis was right when he said, " *Christianity, if false, is of no importance, and if true, of infinite importance. The only thing it cannot be is moderately important.* "[24]

God is "all in" for us. He has given everything we need for life and godliness. He simply wants us to be "all in" for Him and love Him in the same manner He loves us.

Frances Ridley Havergal, the British musician, and devotional writer, left us such classic hymns as "Like a River Glorious," "Who is on the Lord's Side?," "I Am Trusting Thee Lord Jesus," and "Take My Life and Let It Be."

One day in January, 1858, while visiting the art museum in Dusseldorf, Germany, she sat down wearily opposite Domenico Feti's picture of Christ under which was this caption: "I Did This For Thee! What Hast Thou Done For Me?"

---

[24] "C.S. Lewis Quotes." *Relics World*, beyondgoodhealthclinics.com.au/7-effective-strategies-to-process-grief/

Deeply moved, Frances scribbled some lines that flashed into her mind, writing in pencil on a scrap of paper.

Reading them over, they did not satisfy her, so she tossed them into the fire, but they fell out untouched.

Some months later, she showed them to her father, who encouraged her to preserve them. Being a musician himself, he even wrote a melody to accompany them. The resulting hymn, "I Gave My Life for Thee," was first published in 1860 and launched Frances Ridley Havergal as a serious composer of hymns. Here are some of the lyrics:

> I gave My life for thee,
> My precious blood I shed,
> That thou might'st ransomed be,
> And quickened from the dead.
> I gave, I gave my life for thee;
> What hast thou given for Me?

Let's join together and make God our highest priority. We can count the costs involved in following Him, the cost of self-denial, bearing the cross, and following Him. Then, let's engage life to "Keep The Light Burning!"

Keep The Light Burning!

ABOUT THE AUTHOR

Dr. Perry Greene might be considered "homeless." He was born in Albuquerque, New Mexico, as the firstborn son of a career Navy Enlisted Man. He and his family lived "coast to coast" and even had a two-year stint in Guantanamo Bay, Cuba, before it was a prison. As a result, he doesn't have a real hometown. He has been living in Yukon, Oklahoma, since 2006, the most extended residence of his life.

As an adult, Dr. Greene spent forty-five years in church ministry and served churches in Kentucky, North Carolina, Tennessee, Texas, Alabama, and Oklahoma. He earned four Bible-related degrees: Bachelor of Science (1976); Master of Arts (1980); Master of Divinity (1985); and Doctor of Ministry (1990). In addition to ministering in various churches, Dr. Greene was an adjunct Bible teacher at Abilene Christian University in Abilene, Texas.

In 2018, Bott Radio honored Greene with the "*Patriot Pastor of the Year*" award. In addition to being a student of scripture, he has an intense interest in the spiritual foundations of America. Perry's goal is to research and reconnect God and America by "telling His story in our history" and making contemporary applications.

Dr. Greene is currently a podcaster, lecturer, and author. After his forty-five years of church ministry, he established his ministry, "God-N-America" (GodNAmerica.com). He has published, *Our U.S. Holidays, Volume 1: Faith, Hope, and Liberty.* Currently, he is working on a "Grief" manuscript, *GodNAmerica,* and *Our U.S. Holidays, Volume 2.*

Index

Made in the USA
Columbia, SC
14 May 2022